Praise for
LORENZO MILANI, THE SCHOOL OF BARBIANA *and the* STRUGGLE *for* SOCIAL JUSTICE

"This cleverly written and sensible book reveals the soul of Lorenzo Milani as manifest throughout his life and action. During the past 46 years, we have seldom had occasion to read such a good and exhaustive summary of the concepts and facts that lie at the heart of Lorenzo Milani's life and human experience. *Hic est aut nusquam quod quaerimus.*"

The 'evergreen' pupils of Don L. Milani,
Don Milani & Barbiana School, Training & Research Center, Vicchio-Florence

"This rare contribution to the literature bears witness to the reasons educators around the globe must work to formidably rethink critical traditions derived primarily from North American theories of schooling. Through skillfully engaging the revolutionary force of Italian educator Lorenzo Milani's pedagogy and the passion of *Lettera a una Professoressa*, Federico Batini, Peter Mayo, and Alessio Surian move us brilliantly toward an international vision of critical pedagogy—a humanizing vision firmly anchored upon the everyday lives of those who most suffer the ravages of capitalism's discontent."

Antonia Darder, Loyola Marymount University, Los Angeles; author of
Culture and Power in the Classroom and *Reinventing Paulo Freire: A Pedagogy of Love*

"The pedagogical work of Lorenzo Milani is original, inspirational, and relevant for today's realities. A radical democratic educator, he used collective writing as critical literacy production with his young students. His ideas and practices certainly deserve more international attention, and this book provides an engaging and thoughtful introduction to them.

Batini, Mayo, and Surian make an important and timely contribution to the field of critical pedagogy. This is a must-read for all those interested in the connections between education and social justice."

Daniel Schugurensky, School of Social Transformation, Arizona State University

LORENZO MILANI, THE SCHOOL OF BARBIANA *and the* STRUGGLE *for* SOCIAL JUSTICE

Narrative, Dialogue, and the Political Production of Meaning

Michael Peters & Peter McLaren
Series Editors

Vol. 1

The Education and Struggle series is part of the Peter Lang Education list.
Every volume is peer reviewed and meets
the highest quality standards for content and production.

PETER LANG
New York • Washington, D.C./Baltimore • Bern
Frankfurt • Berlin • Brussels • Vienna • Oxford

FEDERICO BATINI, PETER MAYO, *and* ALESSIO SURIAN

LORENZO MILANI, THE SCHOOL OF BARBIANA *and the* STRUGGLE *for* SOCIAL JUSTICE

PETER LANG
New York • Washington, D.C./Baltimore • Bern
Frankfurt • Berlin • Brussels • Vienna • Oxford

Library of Congress Cataloging-in-Publication Data
Batini, Federico.
Lorenzo Milani, the School of Barbiana, and the struggle for social justice /
Federico Batini, Peter Mayo, Alessio Surian.
pages cm. — (Education and struggle: narrative, dialogue,
and the political production of meaning; vol. 1)
Includes bibliographical references and index.
1. Catholic Church—Education—Italy—History—20th century.
2. Milani, Lorenzo. 3. Poor children—Education—Italy—History—20th century.
4. Popular education—Italy—History—20th century.
5. Scuola di Barbiana (Barbiana, Italy)—History.
6. Social justice—Italy. I. Mayo, Peter. II. Surian, Alessio. III. Title.
LC506.I8B38   371.071'20945—dc23   2013024567
ISBN 978-1-4331-2153-1 (hardcover)
ISBN 978-1-4331-2152-4 (paperback)
ISBN 978-1-4539-1194-5 (e-book)
ISSN 2168-6432

Bibliographic information published by **Die Deutsche Nationalbibliothek**.
Die Deutsche Nationalbibliothek lists this publication in the "Deutsche
Nationalbibliografie"; detailed bibliographic data is available
on the Internet at http://dnb.d-nb.de/.

© 2014 Peter Lang Publishing, Inc., New York
29 Broadway, 18th floor, New York, NY 10006
www.peterlang.com

All rights reserved.
Reprint or reproduction, even partially, in all forms such as microfilm,
xerography, microfiche, microcard, and offset strictly prohibited.

Contents

Preface by Roger Dale   vii

CHAPTER 1.
    Introduction: Lorenzo Milani's Relevance to Our Times   1

CHAPTER 2.
    Don Milani and His Time   10

CHAPTER 3.
    Lorenzo Milani and the School of Barbiana's Pedagogical Approach   50

CHAPTER 4.
    Writing as Collective Literacy   81

Notes   105

References   115

Name Index   123

Subject Index   125

Preface

Several years ago, in the middle of a typically stimulating conversation with my good friend, Peter Mayo, he referred to the *Letter to a Teacher* (*Lettera a una Professoressa,* henceforth the *Lettera*), and asked me if I was aware of it. I think he was possibly rather surprised when I told him that not only was I aware of the book, but that, at the beginning of the 1970s, I had been part of a UK Open University sociology of education course team that had made it a set text for students. We were both as delighted as we were surprised, and an invitation to write the Preface for this most interesting volume is the latest outcome of that original conversation.

These origins mean that this piece will necessarily reflect that rather partial understanding of many of the themes covered in the volume. However, the richness and significance of the *Lettera* continue to shine, assisted by the work of the many contributors referred to in the Introduction.

The continuing interest in the *Lettera*, from a range of points of view, demonstrates that the book has considerable contemporary as well as historical significance. However, I do not mean this in a clichéd, 'nothing new under the sun' way. Rather, it is to indicate elements of the importance of the book even when the conditions that had provided such a welcoming context for it on publication have effectively disappeared. Those conditions included vigorous debates around both the nature of education, which in England took the form of 'progressive education,' and the change from selective towards comprehensive entrance to secondary education, about both of which the *Lettera* had something original and significant to contribute. More broadly, we were still in the era of the Cold War and of the ideological battles which it spawned, which, as the *Lettera* showed, took on rather different hues in Italy—and Southern Europe more broadly—particularly through the possibilities of relationships between Catholicism and Socialism.

For me, there are two main aspects of those different contextual conditions where the *Lettera* remains prominent. On the one hand, the significance of the relationships between the ideas expressed in and through education, and the goals (especially those relating to social justice) remain as crucial as ever. On the other, a central feature of the *Lettera* is that they are addressed to *parents,* and here we find almost no parallels between the two epochs.

In terms of the first of these, we find differences in both the central meanings and the nature of social justice, and how it might be attained though education. Despite the differences of interpretation, at the time of the publication of the *Lettera*, and pervading its text, there was still a sense that a properly oriented and organized state education system was a key means to bringing about significant social change, especially through changes in both the role and the distribution of education. To put it rather too simply, it was assumed that this project would deliver social justice in its wake. And maybe the current emphasis on, and centrality of, social justice in itself is one major reflection of the failure of the social democratic goals and processes of the 1970s. In terms of the substance of social justice, following Nancy Fraser, it is not now possible to ignore the expansion of the aspects of social justice to include recognition and representation as well as the implicit redistribution on which the *Lettera* rested (where 'class' had been *the* key status, rather than one *identity* among many). And even these face a challenge from, for instance, Enrique Dussel's proposed substitution of *Liberté, Egalité, Fraternité,* by Liberation, Alterity and Solidarity.

As far as the contribution of schooling to the attainment of social justice goals goes, it is notable that the writers of the *Lettera* focus strongly on the role of the curriculum (and indeed, this may have been one of the reasons for its adoption for the Open University course, since the main text for the course was M. F. D. Young's *Knowledge and Control,* which emphasized the class basis of the selection of school knowledge). Nevertheless, as this volume shows, there was quite sufficient material to make the *Lettera* an extremely significant resource for the development of a critical pedagogy, which did enable a move beyond the curriculum as the crucial area of educational contestation.

However, when we come to consider the changes in the roles of parents since the *Lettera* was written, we do find rather more severe caesurae. The differences I notice may be at least as cultural/spatial as administrative/organizational. They involve the shifts of parents as a group from the cooperative pursuit of collectively determined and mutually beneficial goals, to making parents into individually mutually competitive drivers of (increasingly more 'private' and less 'public') systems of selection and stratification of access to the (increasingly narrowly defined) benefits of compulsory education. This may prove one of the most deeply embedded obstacles to the possibility of the emergence of democratic and egalitarian education systems and experiences.

While it is useful to be able to point to the continuing similarities between what is described and critiqued by the schoolchildren of Barbiana and what continue to be the experiences of children in contemporary schools (and the systems within which they are enmeshed), it would also seem entirely appropriate to try to learn from the continuities and discontinuities, both empirical and ideological, that they reveal. Take, for instance, one of the more vivid and often quoted phrases from the *Lettera*: 'school is a hospital that tends to the healthy and neglects the sick.' For while the phrase certainly retains its vividness and impact when taken alone, as it often seems to be, it loses its key nuances and contemporaneity, when it is detached from the argument to which it is a clinching conclusion. That argument suggests that while we are all aware of the problems caused for other learners by 'trouble makers,' or 'slow' children, for instance, that does not justify disregarding their presence or their particular needs and interests; it is that particular dereliction that would make schools into 'hospitals that tend for the healthy and neglect the sick.' And, as in the case of parents, the definitions of 'healthy and 'sick' persist as if unchanged, with no recognition of the changing meanings and connotations attaching to them, especially as these relate to conceptions of democratic and egalitarian partnership.

Finally, what for me the *Lettera* provides above all, is a resource of hope, against T. S. Eliot's pessimistic conservative surrender, that there could be no hope, 'for hope would be hope for the wrong thing.'

Roger Dale
July 2013

1

Introduction

Lorenzo Milani's Relevance to Our Times

Critical Pedagogy

This year we celebrate the 90th anniversary of the birth of an educator who provides insights for the development of a social justice–oriented education. In his work, and that of his students in two obscure Tuscan localities, we discover many ingredients for a genuine, internationally inspired critical pedagogy. Critical pedagogy refers to the movement of educators, learners, and other cultural workers who derive their inspiration primarily from Paulo Freire, but its origins can be traced to the ideas and work of a number of thinkers and educators in North America. An indication of the range of thinkers involved is provided by the electronic site of the Paulo and Nita Freire International Project of Critical Pedagogy.[1] We immediately come across the names and profiles of educators such as Henry Giroux, Deborah Britzman, Michael Apple, Ira Shor, bell hooks, Donaldo Macedo, Shirley Steinberg, Joe Kincheloe, Peter McLaren, and Antonia Darder. To these we would add, remaining within the North American fold, the recently deceased Roger I. Simon and Paula Allman (Allman was a U.S. citizen, originally from Chicago, but spent most of her academic life in Nottingham, England). Among the historical figures who have provided inspiration, we come across John Dewey, Paulo Freire, Antonio Gramsci, Lev Vygotsky, W. E. B. Du Bois, and, more recently, the Basque educator Jesus "Pato" Gomez. Here the range of figures becomes truly international, and once we break away from the Anglo–North American stranglehold on the field, the sources become numerous and variegated and include Lorenzo Milani, as we strive to underline throughout this text.

Other Italian Pedagogues

Lorenzo Milani is not the only Italian who has a lot to offer to critical pedagogy. Apart from Gramsci, who has gained international cult status among the Left worldwide—more so outside than inside his home country, alas—and possibly the contemporary Giorgio Agamben, who is becoming a constant source of reference in the work of such critical pedagogy exponents as Henry Giroux, we would mention a number of educators/activists in this regard. We would mention Mario Lodi, given adequate treatment in this text especially with regard to the development of collective writing (see Chapter 4). We would also highlight the work of Danilo Dolci (Castiglione, 2004), who combined community learning with action through the "reverse strike" (*sciopero alla rovescia*) and hunger strikes as well as mobilization activities in Sicily, especially in Partinico near Palermo. Then we would also point to Aldo Capitini (Associazione Amici di Aldo Capitini), an antifascist peace educator (especially during the period of fascist rule in Italy) and activist who organized numerous educational and social mobilization activities giving rise to the famous Perugia-Assisi peace walks and the post–World War II Centres for Social Orientation (*Centri di Orientazione Sociale*, or COS) in Umbria and beyond. These were effectively adult education centers for grassroots democracy (*omnicrazia*). Capitini had collaborated with Lorenzo Milani at Barbiana. In November 1960 they launched the first of four issues of the *Giornale Scuola* magazine to be distributed in the Umbria region, although it was mailed to subscribers in the whole of Italy. It was intended to empower workers by focusing on issues of power relations and by using a language accessible to them.

The children's books published since 1951 by Gianni Rodari, and his pedagogical work *Grammatica della fantasia* (1973, The Grammar of Fantasy) had a major impact on educators who encouraged play and creative thinking and considered "mistakes" a source of learning and lateral thinking. *The Grammar of Fantasy* came out of Rodari's collaboration with the learner-centered educational experience practiced in the infant-toddler preprimary school centers managed by the Reggio Emilia Municipality since the 1960s. Such an experience developed into the Reggio Children Foundation, which is instrumental in disseminating Reggio's active pedagogical approach and milestone works by one of its founding members, Loris Malaguzzi, the editor of *Esperienze per una nuova scuola dell'infanzia* (1971, Practices towards a New Pre-primary School), *I cento linguaggi dei bambini* (1995, The Hundred Languages of Children), and the *Zerosei* and later *Bambini* magazines. (see Hoyuelos Planillo, 2004)

International Following

It is, however, with Lorenzo Milani and his students that this contribution to the critical pedagogy literature is concerned. There are places in various parts of the world where Milani and the School of Barbiana are synonymous with *critical education*, to use the more internationally diffuse word, rather than *critical pedagogy*, which retains a North American and perhaps even British ring. Their work is lauded in Spain as our references in the text at hand to the writings of theology professor José Luis Corzo Toral (2008) at Salamanca would indicate. In 1982, the Movimiento de Renovación Pedagógica de Educadores Milanianos (MEM; Milanian Educators' Movement of Pedagogical Innovation) was founded in Spain. In 2012 it included a network of 71 members, 219 regular subscriptions to their *Educar (NOS)* journal, and an average of 1,085 readers. Since 1997 they have been cooperating with the UNESCO Associated Schools Programme.

Over the years Milani's work has also made inroads into the Canadian center of critical pedagogy that is the Ontario Institute for Studies in Education (OISE), the University of Toronto's graduate school of education; Edmund O'Sullivan (personal email correspondence with Peter Mayo) states that the term *critical pedagogy* was coined there during a conference bringing together persons who were to become some of the major exponents of the field. One of the three authors of our book had given a brownbag seminar in 2005 on Milani and critical leadership at OISE's Centre for Leadership and Diversity. Milani's ideas are now being promoted there primarily through the efforts of academic and teacher educator John P. Portelli (a contributor to critical pedagogy), although there had been an important resource website connected with Milani's work and the School of Barbiana's celebrated *Letter to a Teacher* that was hosted by Daniel Schugurensky during his days as an academic at this Toronto institution. Schugurensky, as we will reveal later on, had read the *Lettera*, the major text cited throughout this book, on the sly during his high school days in Argentina. And yet this episode will reveal how a Spanish version of the text was stealthily doing the rounds in this Latin American country and, we would assume, other Spanish-speaking countries, many of which were then under fascist rule.

Many of Milani's ideas derive from different stages in his own trajectory from a member of one of Florence's wealthiest and most prestigious families, via a stint in an art academy as a prospective artist, to his conversion to Catholicism and taking up holy orders, renouncing his family wealth and privileges in the process. He took up and lived the vow of poverty and engaged in battles, including education as a form of struggle, on the side of the oppressed.

The *Lettera* and Other Texts

Commentators on Milani's work devote great importance to the *Lettera*, given its stature as a text that captures some of the basic features of a socially differentiating education within a Western democracy as well as providing insights for a truly transformative and possibly revolutionary pedagogy geared toward the kind of outcomes one would expect any citizen to achieve (the acquisition of "powerful knowledge" that any bourgeois parent would expect for her or his child) but which extended beyond this. It is the kind of pedagogy that can contribute to the creation of a caring society, a society predicated on a culture of social justice. In this regard, it provides much more than the kind of education generally made available to members of the ruling classes. This pedagogical approach is intended to enable its adherents to place their knowledge, including knowledge and insights derived through critical engagement with texts and episodes, at the service of others. It is the kind of knowledge capable of enabling the hitherto downtrodden to become sovereign citizens, perhaps gradually morphing from a "class in itself" (*klasse in sich*) to a class for itself (*klasse für sich*), if we are allowed to use Marx's terminology, which Milani would probably have been careful to avoid.

Despite his commitment to the Christian faith and his theological consistencies in this regard, Milani provides much grist for anyone seeking insights for a critical pedagogical approach to education irrespective of whether one holds religious beliefs or not. This view is reinforced by the fact that Milani himself was not keen on providing religious instruction and was more concerned with helping raise the critical educational level of the peasant and working classes, even setting up a nondenominational school in one of the two localities in which he was involved. As De Salvo (2011) highlights, Milani's pedagogical priority was to promote autonomy and critical thinking. At the same time, he was concerned with the plight of the downtrodden. According to his reading of the Gospels, it is to these people that the Church needs to reach out. This explains his option for the oppressed and his commitment to living a life that is not removed from the reality of these people. It is this that renders his work on education and broader pedagogical politics a "pedagogy of the oppressed" and therefore akin to that of fellow left-wing Christian Paulo Freire. If religious concerns lie at the heart of Milani's pedagogical approach, this was all in keeping with a conception of a Church committed to the poor rather than the dominant classes. Well before the Vatican II Council, Milani had been espousing a conception of the Church on the lines of that referred to by Cornel West and Paulo Freire, as well as others, notably Gustavo Gutierrez, Leonardo Boff, Evaristo Arns and Frei Betto, as the "prophetic church." This stands in contrast to the "Constantinian Church," the "Church of Empire." His pedagogical and social insights can therefore be as inspiring to critical pedagogy as the insights from Liberation Theology. They are imbued with a "language of critique" and a "language of possibility," as Henry Giroux so eloquently argued in his introduction to one of Paulo Freire's books (Giroux, 1985) in which the notion of a Prophetic as opposed to a Traditional or Modernizing Church is discussed.

In Milani's educational work, including that with the children and adolescents at Barbiana, importance is attached to issues connected with race and social class, at times as difficult to separate as the water from the grape juice inside the wine, to adopt a metaphor from Frei Betto (in Borg and Mayo, 2007, p. 39). This emerges quite clearly in their exposition of the socially discriminating nature of bourgeois institutions including parliament and the schools, relations between the global north and south, and issues concerning cultural-technological transfer. Importance was attached at the School of Barbiana to the collective dimensions of learning and action (reading the word and the world critically and collectively, as well as their construction through the mass media); the importance of peer tutoring and the sharing among teacher-learners of frameworks of relevance; reading collectively and critically what is written in the media and responding, also collectively and critically; the existential basis of learning—moving from the occasional to the profound motive; combining academic with technical knowledge and learning; learning knowledge in depth and extensively, never losing sight of its socially contextual basis and its immanent features; placing emphasis on dialogical exchanges within the context of a rigorous approach in which mastery of the area is achieved; placing the emphasis on sound research and preparation and eschewing any laissez-faire pedagogy. These are some of the characteristics of the Milani approach to pedagogy.

Learning History in an Age of Militarization

There is also, in this approach, a strong and relevant (contemporary-wise) element of antiwar pedagogy, developed in the context of a conscientious objection to military service. This involves a thorough and well-researched reading and interpretation of history—against the grain—that connects this aspect of Milani and the pupils' work with that of some contemporary writings concerning the growing culture of militarization and the "carceral state." These feature prominently among the issues expounded on, once again, by Giroux and others—shades of Abu Ghraib, Guantanamo Bay, the torture ("enhanced interrogation techniques") settings in Egypt and other parts of the world (Giroux, 2010). Asked what Don Milani would tell us about recent imperialist wars, especially the infamous wars in Iraq, Edoardo Martinelli, one of the students who wrote the *Lettera*, responded:

> He would only alter his use of words, using those that provide the key to our reading of today's world, words such as limit, expand, survive, etc. As a matter of fact: If the great migrations lead us to cultural expansion, pollution and the impoverishment of the earth compel us to limit consumption and production in order to survive.
>
> War has brought about incoherence and lawlessness. Few make the effort to understand the conspiracies, motives and webs of the oil magnates in the so-called democratic front (Bush) and the terrorist front (Bin Laden). This is where Lorenzo the educator would place the emphasis. He would go about this task in the manner he went about the task then, invoking the sad violent historical experiences of the previous century, demystifying situations and reducing them to their bare essentials. He would remind us of the answer provided to an interviewer by Stangl, the commander of the extermination camp in Treblinka, Poland, where around 20,000 people were gassed and burnt in 24 hrs. "We needed the Jews' money…do you have any idea of what sum we are talking about? That's how steel was bought in Sweden."
>
> A rereading of this interview sends shivers down one's spine since one feels that one is listening to the same kind of talk overheard in bars during the time of the bombardments in Afghanistan and Iraq when everything was bombarded with "intelligence," including women and children—a situation marked by the insensitivity of the opulent west. Everything was legal and continues to be so provided that it serves to reduce the cost of our holidays spent driving around. I must remind you that all this boils down to profit and not passion or ideals—let's be clear. (in Borg and Mayo, 2007, pp. 120–121)

This rereading of history against the grain by Milani and his students would enable us to develop a pedagogical politics relevant to this age of casino-capitalism (Milani's denunciation of hyper-consumption practices in the booming economy of his time can be read as a foreboding with regard to today's "debtocracy" and the Wall Street debacle). Their writings provide us with examples of what Peter McLaren (2005) would call a "pedagogy against empire." "Empire" is here being given a more contemporary meaning, which we associate with the work of Toni Negri, another prominent Italian enjoying recognition outside his own country, and his American colleague, Michael Hardt.

Anticipating/Complementing Critical Sociology of Education

There are affinities between Milani's work and that of Freire. They are both eclectic and inspired by the Gospels. The difference lies in their attitude and embracing of Marxist ideas. And yet Milani is on record as stating, in a letter to a young Prato communist, that he would join forces with communists in fighting against the rich on behalf of the poor but would part company the moment this struggle achieves its aim. Given the likelihood that this is an ongoing struggle, one would be tempted to argue that this means that such a parting was never likely to occur as the goal will never be reached—but that is perhaps bordering on cynicism on our part. Unfortunately, we live in a world in which this cynicism is rife. We therefore need to be imbued with the sense of grounded optimism that both Milani and Freire possessed and conveyed.

Gramsci seemed to have exerted some influence at Barbiana. His texts, notably letters and notes from prison, were set readings at the school, as were Gandhi's biography, the Gospels, Socrates' *Apologia* (via Plato), the letter of the Hiroshima pilot, writings by Thornton Wilder, and many others. And yet Marxism and Marx himself, for example, are conspicuous by their absence in the *Lettera,* despite the fact that this book evokes the kind of situation that calls out for a Marxist class analysis. Yet who is to say that insights from this literature were not at the back of the authors' minds when producing a volume that, in effect, is free from the kind of references we would find in texts dealing critically with bourgeois, capitalist politics? This kind of politics is the target of the students' attack in their critique of public schooling in the *Lettera* and their castigation of the culture of militarization in the other famous letters. One would also include here Milani's never-ending critique of the consumer-culture ideology. What we are presented with is a devastating set of critiques of capitalism and its eclipsing of a genuine democracy.

The Gospels, or rather a reading of them from the standpoint of the oppressed, the lowest positioned socially (*gli ultimi*), were the major source of inspiration. And yet, we would reiterate that, at his behest, his classes at San Donato were devoid of religious symbols, to render them non-confessional and therefore secular.

Despite the lack of visible Marxist influences in Milani's work, the writings in the *Lettera* and *Esperienze Pastorali* (*Pastoral Experiences*) anticipate or complement the arguments submitted by French and U.S. philosophers and sociologists, some Marxist or neo-Marxist, concerning the role of bourgeois formal education in the process of social and cultural reproduction. The following come to mind:

Louis Althusser, Nicos Poulantzas, Christian Baudelot and Roger Establet, Samuel Bowles and Herbert Gintis, Jean Anyon, Pierre Bourdieu, and Jean Claude Passeron. The convergences between Milani's writings, or those written by the Barbiana students under his direction, and those of the French anthropologist/sociologist Pierre Bourdieu (no Marxist), with respect to the school and bourgeois "cultural capital," are uncanny. It seems as though Milani, an avid reader of French literature, was exposed to the kind of critique of bourgeoisie culture and power that emerged from France during his time and that certainly influenced Bourdieu; the Frenchman's work also constitutes an integral part of this body of critical literature.

Milani was not without his contradictions. Enthusiasm for the work of any figure must be tempered by a consideration of these contradictions lest we engage in hagiography, something we are hoping to avoid in this text. These indications of apparent contradictions are interspersed throughout the text and give rise to certain considerations such as those regarding the limits to one's ability to extricate oneself from one's skin and the conditioning of one's *habitus*. We are also wary not to provide a non-historical reading of statements, constantly bearing in mind the contextual specificities that led to their emergence in the first place. The following chapter, focusing on Milani's times, was partly written with this purpose in mind.

Antidote to Measuring Schools

There is ample material in Milani's corpus of writings and that of his students to provide the basis for a process of education that serves as an alternative to the prevailing one—the kind of education that surrounds us at present that is predicated on excessive competitive individualism with the separation between students supposedly occurring on the basis of merit when it, in effect, constitutes a process of social selection as a result of which materially rewarding power is retained by those who already wield it at the expense of the majority (the minority-majority divide broadens considerably in this age of speculative financial capitalism, as the movement of the 99% has been indicating). It provides an antidote to the prevailing contemporary system characterized by testing, standardization, league tables, vouchers, "performativity" in Lyotard's sense (everything translates to easily quantified measured outcomes), a false notion of "choice," and inequitable decentralization policies.

When the *Lettera* was published in 1967, it served as a clarion call for those participating in what came to be known as the '68 movement. Intellectuals connected with that period, such as Pier Paolo Pasolini and Mario Capanna, waxed lyrical about it. It was subsequently published in the United States in 1970, the same year as the English version of *Pedagogia do Oprimido* (Pedagogy of the Oppressed) and Ivan Illich's *Deschooling Society*. Although parts of it featured in key radical texts, even a key text on radical adult education in the early 1980s, it seems to have had less of an impact than the other two works, especially Freire's.

Rekindling Interest in Milani in a Period of Indignation

One wonders whether this book about Milani, following shortly on another English translation and annotated version of the *Lettera*—which we will be using as the main source for quotes in English from this important work (Borg, Cardona, and Caruana, 2009)—in addition to other primary sources for Milani's work, notably all texts in Italian and Burtchaell's (1988) translation of the *Letter to the Military Chaplains* and the *Letter to the Judges*, would help rekindle an interest in Milani's work. The time seems ripe for this. The main sources can serve as "manifestos," just as they did in 1968, for those movements worldwide that have provided a groundswell of mobilization against a capitalist system that has seriously shortchanged ordinary human beings. These works strike us as inspirational for the global politics of indignation and quest for genuine popular democratic renewal that characterize our times. We must temper our eagerness to brandish these texts as manifestos with the sobering consideration that the Barbiana experience started and ended at Barbiana. These texts provide no templates, no recipe to be transferred across historical and geographical contexts. In this, Milani anticipates Freire who argued that experiments cannot be transplanted but must be reinvented. And yet we have seen enough reinvention among those who joined the Occupy movements throughout the world to make us believe that Milani's ideas, as revealed earlier by Martinelli, can have relevance for present-day struggles. They can constitute yet another resource of hope on which these movements and all those striving for social change can draw.

2

Don Milani and His Time

His Education and Conversion: The Years of Fascism

> They presented the Empire to us as the glory of the Homeland! I was 13 years old. It feels like yesterday. I jumped for joy for the Empire. Our teachers had forgotten to tell us that the Ethiopians were better than us. That we went and burnt their huts with their women and children inside, when they hadn't done anything to us. That vile school, consciously or unconsciously I don't know, was preparing us for the horrors that were to come three years later. They were preparing millions of obedient soldiers. Obedient to Mussolini's orders. To be more precise, obedient to Hitler's orders. Fifty million dead.
> —Lorenzo Milani, *Letter to the Judges*

Lorenzo Milani's life story is set during an eventful historical period whose numerous social and political events were to define the Italy of the time. The events that intersect with Don Milani's life span from the end of fascism to the student movement of 1968.

Milani was born at a time when fascism was coming to power. In 1921–1922 the Bonomi government was riddled with contradiction. This was the season in which the ruling liberal classes and Giolitti's political project were to definitively fail. When the first Mussolini government won the vote of confidence in November

1922 it signalled the growing importance of extra parliamentary power and decision-making centers, for which parliament began to assume the sole purpose of ratification. In fact, when Mussolini was first called on to form a new government, he was head of a party that had only 35 MPs. The king was so strongly influenced by the ruling classes (major landowners, industrialists, the judiciary, and high state authorities) that he embraced the idea of a Mussolini government. The liberal state failed because it believed that the man of rule heading a strong government was merely a parenthesis that would later have been normalized in parliament, thus reviving the strength and future prospects of the liberal area. This was the early fascist period, the phase "between 1922 and 1925/6, defined by an increasingly authoritarian use of liberal parliamentary institutions," while in the "later phase party pluralism and parliamentary institutions were suppressed, giving way to a system of dictatorship and the establishment of a one party state" (Salvadori, 1994, pp. 56–57). The 1924 elections were held according to the voting law demanded by the fascists (the law gave two thirds of all seats to the party that won more than 25% of the vote). The elections were dominated by violence, fraud, and intimidation, thus allowing the electoral roll made up of fascist, liberal, nationalist, and moderate Catholic candidates to reach its desired objective, giving the fascist party control over the country. (Unable to comprehend the gravity of the historical moment, the opposition parties went to the elections split up into six different electoral rolls.) The well-known Giacomo Matteotti affair saw the socialist MP kidnapped and killed by fascist emissaries on June 10, 1924, after having exposed the widespread illegality of the elections to parliament. Opposition parties reacted by abandoning parliament,[1] yet despite the moral force of the statement the king did not deny his vote of confidence to Mussolini as the antifascists had hoped. As a result, not only did Mussolini immediately regain control of the situation, but on January 3, 1925, he publicly assumed responsibility for what had happened. The situation was not easy: the head of government had admitted responsibility for having eliminated a member of the opposition; every vestige of democracy had completely disappeared, and legality had effectively been suppressed. Mussolini's speech on January 1925 is generally taken to represent a watershed in Italian history, marking the beginning of the real fascist dictatorship.

Lorenzo Milani was born into a well-off, middle-class family on May 27, 1923. Thanks to their numerous farm holdings the family had lived on independent means for generations, becoming a family of intellectuals and academics. During his childhood, however, the 1929–1930 depression forced his father, Adriano Milani Comparetti (once a university lecturer),[2] to find work as a manager, and the family moved to Milan.

In the meantime, the reconciliation between State and Church (which was to heal the 1870 rift caused when the newly born Italian monarchy "took" Rome, prerogative of the Pope until that time) had restored strength, international prestige, and internal legitimization in the eyes of the Catholics to the fascist regime. In fact, the 1929 Concordat, known as the Lateran Treaty and signed by the Italian State and the Vatican, recognized papal sovereignty over the Vatican, made religious education obligatory in elementary and middle schools, recognized Catholicism as the official state religion in Italy, and invested marriages performed by the Catholic Church with civil validity.

On June 29, 1933, although they weren't religious, the Milanis married in the church and baptized their three children to avoid problems with fascism due to the obviously Jewish origins of Lorenzo Milani's mother, Alice Weiss.[3] The farsightedness of his parents was proved in 1938 when fascism introduced discriminatory laws against the Jews, although open discrimination against all non-party members was already practiced (membership was obligatory for many professions).

Between the ages of 10 and 14 Lorenzo was often ill due to an eye condition. In this period fascism was cultivating its colonialist ambitions. In 1935 the Italian aggression against Ethiopia—the only African country that had maintained independence—was conducted with offensive weapons banned by international conventions (suffocating gas) and involved the large-scale employment of forces. With the occupation of Ethiopia on May 6, 1936, Mussolini announced the creation of the East African Italian Empire made up of Somalia, Eritrea, and Ethiopia. Italy's aggression earned condemnation from the Society of Nations, but sanctions against the country were limited to the blocking of a few economic provisions and had little effect. On the other hand, the so-called unjust sanctions consolidated patriotic feeling in the country and consensus for the regime reached a peak. Benedetto Croce himself adhered to the "Gold for the Homeland" initiative (to support military costs) by handing in his medal as Senator of the Realm. Shortly after, in December 1937 Italy blatantly abandoned the Society of Nations, landing the final blow to its international authority and powers of mediation.

The education that Milani received at home, a cultured environment, attentive to art, full of books and frequented by intellectuals, was greatly superior to the education he received from the fascist school system (see the opening quote). Lorenzo was never a model student; he suffered from boredom and found respite in amusements with his classmates: "At school he did fairly badly: 5/10 in History, Ancient Greek and written Latin; 4/10 in Philosophy and poor in Religion. At home he repeatedly complained that he wanted to stop wasting time and getting bored in a class that was lost in idleness and terror during oral exams. On insistence from his parents he agreed to continue on one condition: that he could pass from the first to the third year of senior high school, skipping the second year entirely (after having taken the necessary exams)" (Sessi, 2008, p. 13). Despite the amazement and disapproval of his teachers he was to pass his exams at the Liceo Berchet Senior High School. In 1934, in line with family tradition, Lorenzo had enrolled in the Berchet school, but had then moved to the Barnabite Zaccaria Senior High School to return later to the former institution.[4] In May 1941 when, like all schools across Italy, his school was closed due to the war, Lorenzo obtained his school leaving certificate on the basis of his last term's results (despite achieving only 8/10 in good behavior). He recalled his schooling in negative terms, as can be seen from the opening quote. Growing up in a cultured, nonreligious, cosmopolitan environment that was respectful of difference and diversity, Lorenzo Milani could not have felt either sympathy or passion for the increasingly narrow-minded school of his adolescence, faithful to fascist party policy and intent on adulating Mussolini.

Then followed a time of fundamental decisions for Lorenzo. He lived for a year in Florence and became an assiduous visitor to the painter H. J. Staude.[5] He told his parents of his desire to devote himself to painting, a desire that his father regarded as a transitory, infantile infatuation; he had hoped that Lorenzo would follow family tradition and enroll at university. Instead, in 1942, he asked to enroll at the Academy of Fine Art at Brera. During the Florentine period an episode had a profound effect on him. While he was painting near Pitti Square in Florence a working-class woman saw him eating a sandwich and rebuked him: "you don't eat white bread in the streets of the poor." The sense of unease that seized him induced him to formulate the conviction that the well-off, wealthy world, of which the Milani family was undoubtedly part, was indebted to the exploited working classes. When he returned to Milan he opened a studio where a study of color in the Catholic liturgy signalled his initial interest in the Church. In 1942 while on holiday at the family house in Montespertoli (near Florence), he found an old book of Mass and wrote to one of his two closest friends at the time, Oreste del Buono: "I'm reading the book of Mass. Do you know that it's more interesting than 'Six Characters in Search of an Author'?" The events of the war forced the Milani family to take refuge in Florence again, and Lorenzo closed his studio in Milan to continue his artistic research from the country home.

His definitive conversion dates to his meeting with Don Raffaele Bensi, who was to become his spiritual father, in June 1943. He was confirmed on June 12, 1943, with Don Raffaele Bensi as his godfather, in a ceremony officiated by Cardinal Elia della Costa, who would also ordain him as priest in 1947. In November 1943 he entered the Cestello seminary where his outspoken, ironic, and defiant character was to provoke conflict with the rector, Monsignor Giulio Lorini, and the general vicar, Don Mario Trapani. In the same month, November 1943, Lorenzo began an exchange of letters with his mother that was to continue until the end of February 1967, just a few months before his death (defying the stereotypes that surround correspondence between Catholic priests and their respective mothers[6]). His family did not support his choice, and none of his relatives was present when he received tonsure. His parents did respect his choice, however, and did their best not to stand in the way of it (Milani, 1997). A letter written from the Seminary on March 14, 1944, is emblematic: "Dear Mother, I'm sorry that my lack of freedom weighs on you, but don't worry about it because it doesn't weigh on me at all. When one freely gives away one's freedom, one is more free than one who is forced to keep it. He who frees himself from his own freedom, frees himself from the weight of carrying it" (p. 22). Lorenzo Milani's time in the Seminary, however, was not a happy one. The Seminary's educational methods clashed with his independent and highly critical behavior, this behavior incurring the hostility of the authorities with whom he never had a good relationship, even in his submission to them.[7] In his letters of this period the war comes across as a distant echo, half seen in the background. It is never at the forefront, never the subject of explicit thought or at least not in any of the material to which we have access.

In contrast with his relationship with the authorities, his relationship with his mother was always one of reciprocal respect for each other's respective beliefs. Lorenzo never asked his mother to convert (explicitly or implicitly[8]); neither did his mother ever try to convince him not to follow his vocation nor to abandon it later when, intent on preserving and supporting the existing conservative order, the Church began to persecute this young priest, advocate of a real social and cultural revolution. The desire to have his mother with him, on the other hand, was often voiced; at times ironic, at times direct, nevertheless he always respected his mother's beliefs, as his countless letters testify:

> How can you think I'm still so narrow minded as to need the priest's mother to go to Church? If you honour me by coming to stay you will never have to go to church and no-one will object because they all know what I think and that I never invite any adults to come. On the contrary, I normally invite them not to come. I've always dreamed that one day you'll come and be with me. You've already seen enough to know that being a mother in law is impossible, as is being a grandmother. You're my mother and from the very beginning I've always planned for you to be with me. I'll make sure you're waited on and honoured from head to toe. I will give up poverty and everything so that you can be with me, and you'll see that you'll be at rest and you can be my spiritual guide, lady of the house and head of the nursery and mixed popular school that we're going to set up in a few years time[9] (Milani, 1997, p. 83).

Don Milani's conversion and its evolution, however, are still surrounded by mystery. "He may have written to Carla, a girl from Milan with whom he had a deep friendship and who he wanted to see before he died" (Sessi, 2008, p. 17), but his letters to her and to Don Bensi remain classified at their request.

Saverio Tutino,[10] another dear friend of those years, remembers the young Lorenzo in this way: "He was so independent inside, such a free spirit. Take school, I diligently carried out my duty, which was a duty towards my parents, so I made sure I was always successful....Lorenzo never seemed to have to answer to anyone, if not to himself. He was never tempted to follow fashion, not even vaguely engaging in antifascist rebelliousness, like reading books and magazines that made us feel independent of the regime's propaganda. He was different from all of us: unconventional and bloody minded, he liked going against the grain. He behaved like he wrote, without paying the slightest attention to punctuation or syntax" (Fallaci, 1993, p. 55).

On July 13, 1947, he was ordained priest, just a few months after the death of his father in March 1947. On August 20 he was provisionally assigned as chaplain to the parish of Montespertoli, but he was unhappy about the assignment because the priest in charge, Don Bonanni, didn't want him to move to the parish. "On Sundays I preach and do catechism but during the week I don't do anything to make him think that I consider myself chaplain" (Milani, 1997, p. 53). In October 1947, after the short interlude at Montespertoli, he was assigned as chaplain to the parish of San Donato in Calenzano. He arrived on October 9, 1947, in the middle of a downpour, as he writes to his mother:

> I've been waiting so many years for this day, not because I want to leave you, but to have a job and earn a living! So I'm happy now and I wish you were too. Yesterday evening I arrived in the middle of a rainstorm but about 15 children and young men were waiting for me in the rain and they led me in a procession right up to the house and then they hung on the bells and rang them full peal to announce the arrival of the long awaited chaplain.

From the beginning of his time at San Donato he ran into dispute, with the other priests. On July 1, 1949, the Holy Office proclaimed a decree regarding the excommunication of Communists and Don Milani, in a regular meeting of the clergy, voiced his opposition:

> referring to common canonical law and the practice of confession...to demonstrate that they had not been detached enough in judging and applying the decree on Communism....And not having anything with which to counter my well prepared arguments, they took refuge in a private meeting with the Cardinal. So I was forced to say to them all: you call him a fool, you know he's a fool and you've always done what you liked, yet now that you have to take responsibility for something you dump it on his shoulders,

all humble and obedient. The most debated point was the denial of marriage. With good solid doctrine I demonstrated that marriage should never be denied. They all said it should and in fact they have denied it. The very next day, in a corner of all the newspapers a short little article appeared, straight and to the point 'Notification of the Curia: never deny marriage.' What a shame that we won't have the next meeting for another 6 months, otherwise I would have had great fun! (Milani, 1997, p. 73).

A few days later, writing to his mother about assisting a dying mother, he commented "And as a good representative of Jesus I'll be careful not to ask them what party they're in" (p. 76).

Nevertheless, the Italian political situation was not easy in those years and Don Milani's opinions, as well as the energy, intransigence, and honesty with which he voiced them, quickly earned him many enemies.

The Italian Political Situation: After Fascism and the Birth of Christian Democracy

The political situation that straddled the fascist years underwent numerous changes. In the Italian fascist period new political parties were formed that were forced undercover until the fall of fascism. With the end of World War II Italians discovered that they could freely participate in political debate, and the Catholics also contributed. The PPI (Italian Popular Party) founded by Don Luigi Sturzo had been disbanded by the fascists in 1926.[11] The new political formation was named DC (the Christian Democrat Party) and was founded in 1942,[12] long before the defeat of the regime in a series of secret meetings held at the house of Enrico Falk, a Catholic Milanese businessman.

Postwar Italy abandoned the monarchy to become a republic and met with gradually increasing prosperity. After the Liberation (on April 25, 1945, the date that marks the end of the war in Italy), Italy was an exhausted country not only weighed down by more than five years of involvement in the world's second major conflict, but also by the hard years of privation imposed by fascism and two years of equally hard Allied and German occupation. The country was scarred by a global conflict, a long period under a totalitarian regime, and a harsh civil war of resistance. Italy was deprived of almost all communication routes. It was only in the autumn of 1945, for example, that the trains connecting Rome with Northern Italy began working again. Fortunately, its factories and electric power stations had not been completely destroyed as the German occupation in the north of the country had turned the industrial triangle into a strategic area used to safeguard the Reich's war economy.

Inflation reached record levels, due to the effect of the Allies' military lira that had been printed to finance the military occupation. Prices rose to 5 times those of 1938; industrial production collapsed by 70% in comparison to the prewar period, and agricultural production dropped by 40%.[13] The center north of the country was defined by widespread antifascism while the majority of those living in the south had not known the harsh reality of the German occupation nor had they experienced the Resistance, and thus monarchical, conservative tendencies prevailed.

The postwar phase in Italy saw a unified, postfascist, national government between 1945 and 1947. Political power was in the hands of the antifascist parties: the Action Party, the Socialist Party (PSI), the Communist Party (PCI), the Christian Democrat Party (DC), and the Liberal Party. The Republican Party was to join them slightly later. The first government, between June and December 1945, was led by Ferruccio Parri from the Action Party and was driven mainly by the intention to punish those responsible for fascist war crimes, as well as the political and moral renewal of the State. The Christian Democrat Party, the Catholic Church, and the Liberal Party, however, were cautious about this program and were well supported by the Allies. The prominence of the Christian Democrat Party was guaranteed by the support of the Allies and the only institution that had survived 20 years of fascism, the Catholic Church. Togliatti, leader of the Communist Party, understood the difficulties of carrying out reforms that were capable of altering the socioeconomic equilibrium of the country. He settled for exercising his influence on policy from within the government, while at the same time maintaining control over the creeping unrest that was spreading as a result of unemployment, inflation, the enthusiasm associated with the end of the war, and the anxiety related to a new world. Togliatti was equally aware that a "revolution" would have been impossible because the Allied forces would have staged an armed intervention, so his strategy was to present the PCI's position within the government as guarantee for the moderates that the social order of the country would not be seriously altered. If, as we will see shortly, Togliatti's project of exercising a growing influence on the government from within was destined to failure, his long-term strategy was rewarded by history as the PCI became the largest and most long-lived communist party in Western Europe.

When the Parri government fell, the leader of the Christian Democrat Party, Alcide De Gasperi, came to power and remained uninterrupted as prime minister until 1953.

The initial situation immediately after the war was one of dialogue between the DC and the PCI, but they later became locked within a confrontation that would be difficult to resolve. Those in government (the DC and its allies) considered the possible coming to power of the opposition parties (at length dominated exclusively by the PCI) as a "socio-political catastrophe," while the PCI felt that the power held firmly in the hands of the DC was an "expression of the political and social domination of the enemy" (Salvadori, 1994, p. 64).

De Gasperi enjoyed the complete trust of the Allies who, after just a few weeks of government, restored the administration of the few remaining regions still under Allied control to the government. The Christian Democrat politician decided to bind Italy even closer to the United States by pursuing an anti-Soviet foreign policy and an anti-communist domestic policy (that also guaranteed him the support of Pope Pius XII). On June 2, 1946, a referendum was held to express preference for the monarchy or the republic and to vote in the members of the Constituent Assembly. For the first time women were given the power to vote.[14] The republic won and the elections for the Constituent Assembly saw the predominance of three major parties: the Christian Democrats, the Communists, and the Socialists. The Action Party, protagonist of the Resistance, obtained an extremely disappointing result and disbanded not long after; some of its members were to join the Socialist Party, while others joined the Republican Party. De Gasperi decided to collaborate with the Communist Party to draw up the Constitution and sign the peace treaty (wanting its onerous consequences to weigh on the shoulders of all parties). On January 1, 1948, the republican Constitution came into effect. In May 1947, however, the Socialist and Communist Parties were forced to leave the government after the ratification of the peace treaty on February 10, 1947, after pressure from the United States and Pius XII. In January 1947 Giuseppe Saragat, socialist leader who opposed the party secretary's policy of alliance with the communists, founded a new party, the Italian Workers Socialist Party, later named the Italian Socialist Democratic Party. Thanks to this split, De Gasperi was able to count on the support of some of the socialists even after the expulsion of the Socialist and Communist Parties from the government. After the agreement with the United States, whose Marshall Plan promised considerable economic aid to the country, De Gasperi expelled the two left-wing parties and became head of a centrist government based on Christian Democracy and the support of minor parties such as the Social Democrat Party, the Liberal Party, and the Republican Party.[15]

Furthermore, from 1947 the liberal economist Luigi Einaudi joined the government as Minister of Budget. Einaudi and his successors (of equally liberal orientation) fought against inflation using traditional methods such as the control of expenditure and investment. They were successful in reversing price trends, but their methods led to serious repercussions such as the curbing of production levels and a staggering rise in unemployment. Such high unemployment resulted in the extenuation of the force of the workers movement. On April 18, 1948, the

Christian Democrat Party won the elections with 48.5% of the total vote, thanks to the effective contribution of the Church (in every parish, churchgoers were warmly invited during mass to vote for the moderate parties). The "people's front," which saw socialists and communists standing together, obtained 35% of the vote. Luigi Einaudi was elected president of the Republic.[16] The transformation was completed in 1949 when Pius XII, advocate of Catholic fundamentalism, pronounced the excommunication of the communists. In 1950 another split, this time originating with the trade unions, further weakened the workers movement. The CGIL trade union was accused of serving communist party policy, thus leading to the birth of the CISL trade union whose members were of Catholic inspiration, and the UIL trade union whose members were social-democrats and republicans.

The anti-communist turn of Christian Democracy was to characterize the early years of postwar republican Italy. One of the main aspects of Catholic political thought was its barely concealed intention to ward off the "socialist threat" (Cristante, 2008, p. 17): the PCI in Italy was one of the largest and well-organized communist organizations in Western Europe, defined by its Marxist origins and its dependence on a Soviet-based frame of reference as well as an important, well-structured presence within local communities (mainly based in popular social centers called "le Case del Popolo").

The Church, on the other hand, was lacerated from within as was its congregation, due to the diverging positions and currents of thought regarding the well-debated question of the relationship between State and Church. Although in theory the question had been resolved by the Lateran Treaty (1929), which established that the two institutions should coexist with respect for the diversity of their roles, many felt, however, that the problem remained unresolved at the practical level.

For the Catholics the Christian Democrat Party seemed to represent an important opportunity to participate in political life, but it found itself in conflict with papal policy, and in the previous decade it had initially ended up splitting along two currents of thought with regard to the international context:

1. The De Gasperi line was in favor of opening up to the West through collaboration between Italy and the United States
2. The Dossetti[17] line, on the other hand, was in favor of a movement toward the Soviet Union and the possibility of dialogue with a world perceived as still very remote.

De Gasperi aimed at "pursuing political autonomy and independence from the church, while making appropriate compromises with civil, secular society" (p. 18), despite remaining close to the Church on many issues. Pope Pius XII, however, had in mind an Italy that was "officially Catholic, led by a party that is just as officially Catholic." This idea was seen as "an improbable utopia in the political field" by De Gasperi who believed instead that it was wiser to present the DC, at least formally, as a political subject that wanted to apply the principles of the Church to politics, without being an incarnation of "the Church's Party." De Gasperi proved to hold the winning line, thus resulting in the consequences outlined above.

In 1954, despite failure to apply the economic development plans presented (one plan was presented by the CGIL in 1949 and one by the Christian Democrat MP Vanoni in 1954 after the death of De Gasperi), the international economy went through an extremely favorable period, resulting in Italy's considerable growth between 1955 and 1963, defined as an "economic miracle" (the average increase in development was between 6% and 8%, not even remotely comparable to the average growth of 2.5% reached in previous years[18]).

The progressive fragmentation of the communist and socialist parties and trade unions led to the long-term domination of the Christian Democrat Party, which also benefited from the "dialectic" position of the Italian Communist Party (as well as the Socialist Party up until 1956, when the PSI's subordination to the PCI came to an end). The PCI continued to maintain an ambivalent attitude toward the parliamentary state, participating and trying to influence its decisions from within, while continuing to interpret its own work within the framework of anticipated revolutionary change.[19]

Ordainment as Priest and the San Donato Years

"One can't explain to a boy why his writing doesn't work if he's never read a book before. All one can do is to advise him to read. Hours of reading for years."—Milani, 1957, p. 184

"So school is as sacred to me as an Eighth Sacrament."—Milani, 1957, p. 203

"After what I've said it isn't difficult to demonstrate that a priest who makes the teaching of the poor his main occupation is doing anything at all foreign to his specific mission (allow me this heresy, now that the more serious fallacy of the priest who devotes himself to recreation has been legitimized)."—Milani, 1957, p. 219

"Children, I promise you in the name of God that I will run this school so as to give you an education and that I will always tell you the truth in everything, whether it honours or disgraces my enterprise."—from an account by Giordano, pupil of the Popular School of San Donato

In the institutional referendum of June 2, 1946, despite conflicting indications from the Cardinal, Lorenzo Milani sided with the Republic. As we have seen, one year later on July 13, 1947, he was ordained priest at the Santa Maria della Scala church. After the short interlude at Montespertoli he was nominated as chaplain in the working-class village of San Donato di Calenzano to assist the old priest Daniele Pugi. It was here that he was to set up the Popular School. When Don Lorenzo Milani arrived at San Donato at just 24 years of age, known as "the baby priest" among the older residents, the parish counted 12,000 inhabitants, almost all of whom were farmers and workers. The majority of the population were workers employed in the ceramics works in Sesto Fiorentino, the Rifredi assembly plants, and the textile industry in Prato where the working day was divided into three shifts. Existing legislation banned women and children from working the night shift (the 3rd shift), but employment laws in Prato were systematically ignored with the complicity of the police and even the judiciary. Don Lorenzo was faced with low levels of general education at San Donato, "yet they certainly weren't inferior to any of the other villages in Tuscany, which did not perform badly in relation to the national average. Most of the young had finished obligatory schooling and had obtained the elementary school leaving certificate, although a few, mostly from farming families, had left school earlier. Hardly anyone went on to high school in Prato or Florence. Many of the adults had not got beyond the second or third year of elementary school and having had very little opportunity to practice in their everyday lives, most of them were to be considered illiterate" (Allievi di San Donato and Lagomarsini, 2008, p. 3). The population, like almost everywhere in central Italy, was highly politicized, and San Donato was split down the middle:

> On the one hand there were the social-communists who represented the vast majority and whose point of reference was the 'Casa del Popolo.' On the other hand there were the Catholics who gathered around the church. Relations between the two groups were icy and tense, characterized by continuous digs, allusions and often real argument (p. 3).

In April 1948 the DC won the election hands down, thanks to the mobilization of the local parishes. Don Milani was to face a series of clashes in both voting rounds, despite having kept to the diktat that required parishioners to vote for the DC. He was to recall the betrayal of that April more than once in the 1950 letter/article to *Adesso* (December 15, 1950, pp. 3–8). The additions he was to make to *Pastoral Experiences* were also memorable. This was the Florentine priest's first book and signalled a real watershed in his human, spiritual, and political life. The appendix was edited a few years earlier, in 1953–1954:

> Four years ago when orders arrived to be strict with the communists I obeyed them. I was hated, abandoned and despised by many of my poor children all for the sake of that decree. I didn't voice a single complaint against the Pope because I knew he was right. But now that I've been working on the cutting edge for the last four years, now that I've painfully clarified mine and the Church's absolute refusal of Marxism to those poor people and I've lost so many of my children, blood of my blood, I don't want anyone telling me I'm a demagogue just because I go looking for lost sheep. I want to be treated like the missionaries. They're allowed to cross oceans and penetrate the jungle and nobody accuses them of acting out of a spirit of adventure....Nobody accuses them of cultivating a passion for the hunt....That's why I have the right to cry out against Baffi and the government. Not for the bread they take away from my children, but for the children they take away from my arms (Milani, 1957, pp. 467–468).

In his letters and in particular in the well-known *Letter to Pipetta*, Don Milani recalled that betrayal:

> It's History turning against me, the 18th April ruined everything, victory was my great defeat. Now the rich have won with my help, I have to admit that you're right, I have to come down to your level and fight the rich. But don't say that's what makes me the only good priest around. You think you please me and instead all you do is rub salt in my wounds. What if History hadn't turned against me? What if April 18th…? You would never have seen me come down to your level to fight the rich. Yes, you're right, you're right, between you and the rich you'll always be right (Milani, 2007b, p. 22).

The San Donato Popular School opened in 1947 as a private evening school. Later a teacher sent by the state would collaborate for five months a year. Slowly the school would extend its timetable and its work until it was open more or less continuously. Almost immediately, Fridays were reserved for talks by special guests that were followed by wide-ranging, lively debates. The themes? Here's how the San Donato pupils remember them: "Some of the subjects tackled in the Friday talks: aeronautics, anatomy, astronomy, art, colonialism, economics, miscarriages of justice, philosophy, newspapers and journalists, child labour, illegal labour, literature, Mafia, medicine, music, Nomadelfia, the death penalty, painting, poetry, politics, criminal law, religion, trade unionism" (Allievi di San Donato and Lagomarsini, 2008, p. 80). Milani wrote dozens of letters to the speakers both before and after their talks to clarify, thank, excuse, comment on the talk, report on how to interact with the children, ask for bibliographical references, remind to send books, invitations to return, and so on.

The reasons behind the decision to open a Popular School can all be found in *Pastoral Experiences,* Milani's most demanding work both in terms of the effort involved in writing it and the length of the book itself:

All of this means that almost the whole of the old aged population and 88.6% of young people are intellectually at the mercy of anyone who has completed a single year beyond elementary school. Before opening one's mouth in front of such a defenceless audience one should put oneself through a long and scrupulous self examination, nurture a delicate and pained respect and recognize in oneself the humiliation of unmerited and excessive power. Has anyone ever talked to our people in this state of mind? Politicians perhaps? Landowners? Traders? Priests? (Milani, 1957, p. 185)....That's why teaching is the only thing I do with conviction for now. It's not that I have blind faith in culture, as if it were some kind of infallible recipe, as if university professors were automatically more Christian than anyone else and had their place in Paradise guaranteed, while the way is barred to the uninitiated....It's just that if they want to, teachers can pick up a New Testament or a Catechism, read it and understand it. Afterwards they can do what the hell they want with it: throw it out of the window or keep it in their heart, get excited by it; if they make the wrong decision then all the worse for them....My school won't turn them into Christians, but it can turn them into men....With this premise I believe I can say that school education, for these people in this moment in time, is not just one of many possible methods, but a necessary measure and an obligatory step (pp. 200–201).

The school, which was set up almost by chance, was not simply part of Don Lorenzo Milani's mission as a priest but the center of his life, and we cannot understand its purpose if we fail to integrate his educational project with his desire for social justice, neither of which are at all separate in his thought: "Rather than bridging the gap of ignorance, we are interested in bridging the gap of difference. By opening our schools, talks and libraries to the middle classes we would fail in the very aim of our work. Do we let the rich come to our soup kitchens?" (Milani, 1957, p. 220).

The Popular School at Calenzano was the basis of Don Milani's educational thought. With his decision to focus above all on lexis and language, he was trying to combat the inability to express oneself and to understand what others say as well as restore a love for one's own education among working-class farmers and workers.

In the San Donato Popular School there were three classes: course A, course B, and course C. The first was for the completely illiterate, the second for those who had reached the third year of elementary school and wanted to pass the final year exams, while the third class was for anyone who wanted to go beyond elementary level. Benito Ferrini, one of the pupils in the early years, describes the experience:

> He insisted on the fact that the only thing us poor people needed was to improve our Italian...and at the beginning we wouldn't believe him. We would ask him to do arithmetic and technical drawing; Gianfranco wanted to learn shorthand because they had told him he'd find a job that way; Mino said he needed square roots for a job in the railways and so on. Don Lorenzo started off on some of these things just to keep us happy and then he would get bored and spend an hour on one word: an insignificant word opened up a whole

world; he would tell us where it came from and how to use it and a thousand different sentences you needed it for and all the different meanings it had and where it could be found in other languages and how it could be used to make other words and how many other words derived from it. It would get to midnight and we still hadn't dipped our pens in our ink and the blank pages of our exercise books were still waiting for the square roots that Don Milani said *he promised we'd do tomorrow*. (Sessi, 2008, pp. 60–61).

As will become clear with his most well-known work, *Letter to a Teacher*, written with his pupils and edited just a few months before his death, his intention was to highlight the class-based nature of the Italian education system in those years, and to do this he introduced the subjects and "cultural values" of the working classes (Bencivinni, 2004), centering his own teaching on oral and written language.

After some initial difficulties the San Donato School met with huge success as Milani (1957) recounts:

The early years of the school were very difficult. We still have difficulties today but we tend to associate them not so much with our youngsters' resistance to school, but with the isolated nature of the experience itself. Our pupils would have a much easier life if they could meet other young people engaged in the same kind of experience at work or within the party, the trade unions or among friends in nearby parishes. After six years the school at San Donato has already made a name for itself, so that according to public opinion the smart ones are those who abandon their play for school and not vice versa, the way people used to think a few years ago (p. 224).

In 1951 Lorenzo Milani fell seriously ill and the Popular School suffered a setback, starting up again in the 1952–1953 school year.

From 25 pupils in 1947–1948, the school reached a total of 81 pupils in 1953–1954, without counting those who Don Milani called "the onlookers," those who only occasionally attended school over the year, bringing the total to 133. In six years the number of pupils increased five times. To get a better idea of Don Milani's progressive effect on the community, it's worth noting that of all the young people between the ages of 14 and 24, only 14% never once came to the school in the seven years that it existed (Milani, 1957, pp. 226–231). Of those who were 11 or 12 when the chaplain first arrived, 100% were to attend his school. Don Milani's analysis of the San Donato experience in *Pastoral Experiences* is painstaking. Rather than stopping at an analysis of attendance, absenteeism, pupil age, or pass and failure rates, he provides a careful and precise analysis of costs and materials used, achievements and also deficiencies.[20]

A full understanding of his educational approach necessitates a careful study of *Pastoral Experiences*, his most complex, articulate, and least-cited work (1957).

As well as providing a real sociological inquiry into the San Donato community and the surrounding area, in the chapter devoted to the Popular School he includes a paragraph titled "I am indebted."

> I owe everything I know to the young workers and farmers I have taught. What they thought they were learning from me, I learned from them. All I did was to teach them how to express themselves while they taught me how to live. They are the ones who informed my thoughts on the things written in this book. I didn't find any of this in my schoolbooks. I learned as I wrote and I wrote because they planted something in my heart. They are the ones who turned me into the priest who they willingly go to school for, who they trust more than their political leaders for whom they would sacrifice anything, and to whom they confess their sins without having to wait until Sunday. I didn't used to be like this and that's why I will never forget what they have given me (Milani, 1957, p. 235).

This is not just the profoundly human recognition of a debt of trust and friendship; Milani's words need to be interpreted literally, constituting one of the high points in his imaginary educational manifesto: learning is co-constructed at the moment in which it takes place; teachers learn at least as much as their pupils, and if they are truly devoted they take full advantage of this incredible experience. Likewise, the embracing of working-class values and culture was not just a mannerism but a real fascination and a profound conviction, as deep-set as his conviction regarding the class-based nature of the state school system. "Italian schools have just one problem. The children who drop out. 462,000 children a year drop out of obligatory schooling along the way. You are the only incompetent ones in school, because you don't go looking for the children you lose" (Milani, 1967). And again, "A selective school system destroys culture, denying the poor any means of expression and denying the rich an understanding of things. The selective school system is a sin against God and against men."

Furthermore, Don Milani's Popular School was not denominational: "In seven years of popular schooling I have never felt there was any need to teach doctrine. And I have never really cared about making edifying or pious speeches. All I do is bide against myself or anyone else talking nonsense and I try not to waste time. I have tried to edify myself, to be as I would like them to become" (Milani, 1957, p. 238). In his many letters Lorenzo Milani often pointed out his sympathy for the liberals, "real liberals," because for opposite reasons, like liberals, he held an absolute indifference to dogma, specifying that true liberals never recalled dogma because they didn't believe in it, while he never remembered dogma for the opposite reason, because he believed in it (Milani, 2007). Another cornerstone of Don Milani's educational thought that emerged during the San Donato period and that is still extremely relevant today is his idea of the educator or teacher. "Often friends ask me how I teach and how I manage to have full classes. They insist that I write down my method for them; that I lay out programs, subjects and educational technique. But they're getting the question wrong. They shouldn't ask about what to do in order to teach but about how one needs to be in order to teach" (Milani, 1957, p. 239). Obviously, Milani's disinterest and even occasional disdain for method need to be contextualized in the historical period, in the figure of Don Milani himself, and in the priority given to other issues. Don Milani's revolution also regarded educational method and more precisely the inclusion of both individual experience and collective working-class culture and farming culture (and later on mountain culture at Barbiana) within his teaching, investing it with the same dignity as that given to the "official" culture (and not just as mere strategy). Many of today's transformations regarding obligatory education and the positive evaluation of children's life experiences and the meanings they bring to them—with the aim of restoring trust in the importance and purpose of education—are deeply rooted in the Milani experience; so much so as to make it easy, sometimes even for Don Milani himself, to draw "best practices" from them. His references to the role and identity of the teacher and educator (the skills necessary to practice this profession, as we would say today), that for more than a century have been excessively dependent on the mastering of subjects (despite the work of Milani and many others), appear absolutely contemporary today[21] if understood and contextualized correctly.

The San Donato Experience and Italian State Schools of the Time

The modernity of the San Donato school and later that of Barbiana, as well as its break with 1950s schooling methods, can be clearly evinced by what his San Donato pupils wrote 50 years after the publication of *Pastoral Experiences:*

> the first thing the school did was to teach us how to live together. Political enemies who swore obscenities at each other turned into people with differing ideas who discussed, respected each other, and expressed their solidarity towards others together....Rather than having a set syllabus, the school was rooted in the local area and looked onto the world through the reading of newspapers and weekly meetings with experts in the most varied subjects. Don Lorenzo often started off his lessons by looking at what was going on in the news, this then led him to address wider considerations and sometimes he had us carry out research projects. This method allowed Don Milani to develop interdisciplinary lessons, involving his pupils in current affairs on a local, national and international level. We addressed social, religious, political, economic and trade union issues which

allowed him to reflect, experiment and analyse together with us, sometimes even assuming public positions on various problems (Allievi di San Donato and Lagomarsini, 2008, p. 76).

The importance of positive relationships and respect, the ability to debate, an interest in current affairs, continuous and active participation, reciprocal collaboration, and writing skills were all at the center of Milani's pedagogy. "The school, attended by believers and atheists, on the one hand aimed to prepare pupils to be free and virtuous men, independent from everyone—priests, communists and masters, Don Milani used to say—and on the other hand to help each one of them discover the ideals, principles, human values—and Christian values for believers—that would become the tracks along which their lives would run" (p. 77).

Twenty years of fascism had destroyed any ambition for pedagogical, sociological, or psychological research that was not in line with the regime, while also keeping any educational literature from abroad at arm's length in case it would "pollute" fascist orthodoxy.[22] Italy only began to feel the influence of active schools, new schools, and the work of Dewey and Makarenko at the beginning of the 1950s.

In those years the Italian state school system had been "reformed" by the Allies.[23] In 1945 the American pedagogue Carleton Walsey Washburne issued the programs that would substitute those introduced by the fascists for nursery and elementary schools. The American pedagogue, a student of Dewey's, had acquired his reputation as head of Winnetka School in Illinois between 1915 and 1943. In 1943 he was nominated as a member of the Allied Control Commission for Italy and, specifically, educational policy adviser to the Italian government. His work began in Sicily and then progressively throughout the areas liberated from German occupation. However, although people were anxious to contribute to the reconstruction of the country, they didn't seem particularly interested in the theme of education (not even the trade unions or the left wing saw the question of education as a priority). In this particularly unusual historical context, Lorenzo Milani's intuition regarding the possibility of emancipation through education and learning should be viewed with real amazement.

Washburne's committee focused on elementary schooling, paying little attention to secondary education. After having met Gino Ferretti, educationalist from the University of Palermo who had never disguised his own antifascism even in earlier years, Washburne handed him the onerous task of drawing up the *Study Programs and Educational Indications for Elementary Schools 1943/44*. The work of this educationalist, which focused on the democratic aims of education, individualization in teaching, an attention to socialization, activation, and the positive evaluation of children's imagination, appears modern for the period. These programs were distributed throughout Sicilian schools but were almost as quickly withdrawn and destroyed. What was the motivation behind this change of mind? Ferretti had not included religious education within his programs and the ecclesiastical authorities made the apostolic delegate to the U.S. government intervene to insist on respect for the Concordat. The following year Washburne, who had moved to Naples, hurriedly set up a new committee that was to include a "Monsignor," as he was to remember himself, to exercise preventative control over the other members so that nothing could be introduced that could be seen as offensive to the Catholic Church. The innovative text that came out in 1945, inspired by the activist theories of John Dewey and permeated by the spirit of democracy, introduced individualized teaching methods, stressed the importance of cooperation and collaboration between pupils, and interpreted the school as a community space open to dialogue with the family and society. However, in looking to find a compromise between modernity and tradition, Washburne was perhaps excessively careful not to hurt the sensitivity of the Catholic Church, mindful of his previous failure with the Sicilian experience. Based on the Concordat regime of 1929, the Church exercised a powerful influence over all primary education, endorsed by the State (religion was considered the foundation and crowning aim of the entire educational process).[24] In the new programs, then, in line with what Don Milani argued, the word as "expression of feeling and thought" was to become central. Traditional methods such as the abuse of premature correction in spelling, syllabification, and choral reading were discouraged, while practices such as observation, the reduction of grammar teaching to a minimum, and its use in ex-post formalization as opposed to its use as a precondition were encouraged. Compromise and backtracking transpired. This time the "Indications for Religious Education" appeared at the beginning of the programs; agricultural work was represented in unrealistic and idyllic terms; the role of the woman was exalted as comforting and useful but rigorously placed within the domestic realm. The *Programs, Instructions and Models for Primary and Nursery Schools* were issued with Ministerial Decree on February 9, 1945, and despite their many compromises they still appeared far too advanced for the Italian context to be fully applied. From the beginning, and with increased force from 1947 after the expulsion of the communists and socialists from government, the Christian Democracy and the Church impeded the effective secularization of the state school system and curbed its development in favor of private and denominational schools. The majority of innovations in the 1945 programs existed only on paper. With the second De Gasperi government that came to power in July 1946, the Ministry for Education was entrusted to the Catholic politician Guido Gonnella, who remained at the helm until 1951.[25]

In this sense the San Donato school resisted the wavering advancements and the more constant backtracking in the state school system. It developed from the outset as a much more modern institution than most state schools, including those involved in the most advanced experimentation.

Words and writing were to be the main interest of Don Milani's entire epic history as a teacher.

At San Donato, then, in the three rooms that were once used exclusively for Sunday School, the extraordinary experience of the Popular School came to life and grew up between 1947 and 1954, coming to a halt after seven years when Don Milani was forcibly transferred to Barbiana. At the end of his stay at San Donato controversy grew. Some accused Don Lorenzo of "playing to the left," while others accused him of "manipulating" his pupils. There were many accusations and almost all of them were whispered behind closed doors, without anyone ever having the courage to confront him, and therefore never giving him the chance to defend himself.

"Some insinuated that he had subjugated us. This is a shameful lie that time has proved wrong. Don Lorenzo tried to provide us with a mind free from any kind of conditioning and a critical but constructive spirit, so much so as to allow us to criticize our very own teacher, who we are proud to have been influenced by" (Allievi di San Donato and Lagomarsini, 2008, p. 79).

The Transfer

> I feel like I'm at the cinema watching the closing scenes of a film with a happy ending. The film with the happy ending is my work at San Donato. I've done everything. I've done the work I wanted to do and I've never been forced into compromise. I'm having great fun in the grand finale. What more could I want? Think of these 5 years as one of my creations. It's not how long it lasts that's important but the fact that it comes to a happy ending. If I can manage to create this kind of ending then I don't have to worry about suffering the torment of regret. Do you remember how Simone Weil answered her boss when he threatened to dismiss her? I've always considered dismissal as the natural crowning of my school career! As far as the date of the final attack is concerned, it's probably been set for the day the Priest in charge dies....Anyway there's no chance of me staying here.—Letter to his mother dated July 14, 1952, Milani, 2007, pp. 101–102.

If further proof was needed of Don Milani's ability to understand and predict, to see beyond single episodes and transitory events, or to comprehend situations and other people's intentions, the above quote provides us with incontrovertible evidence. Lorenzo Milani was convinced that he would eventually be transferred two years before it happened. He knew that he was seen as out of place, an obstacle and a hindrance, "an out of tune bell" as a high prelate was to define him.

The facts are missing on one side: we know an enormous amount about what Don Lorenzo was thinking and working on in this period, while our knowledge is fragmentary with regard to what was going on in the Florentine Curia in the same period and what led them to the conclusion that a "punitive" transfer was necessary.

In 1951, Don Milani was invited to leave San Donato for a few days—he took advantage of the invitation to travel to Germany, warmly encouraged by his mother—so as to soothe the tensions that had arisen as a result of the indications he had given during the local elections. The Florentine Curia had warmly supported the alliance between Catholics and moderates to contrast the advance of the left-wing parties. Don Milani, on the other hand, maintained that the Bishops' decree should be interpreted literally,[26] therefore providing indications during mass on May 11 and 27, 1951, to vote exclusively for Catholic candidates.[27] He immediately received orders to hold his tongue and report to Cardinal Dalla Costa, who reprimanded him for his risky behavior, although it could not be defined as wrong. His mother's advice was fundamental in this period. She, an atheist, opposed his temptation to go public and reveal the Cardinal's orders: "a son mustn't reveal his father's misery in public" (metaphorically speaking of his superior as his father). This is what brought Lorenzo to rush onto a train for Germany, coming back just in time to place his voting paper in the ballot box.

Lorenzo Milani's political position in this period is well summarized by Bencivinni (2004): "The priest must criticize the mistakes of the government and the DC if he is to be believed by the working class when he criticizes the communists; furthermore he must give indications to vote for the DC, advising voters to choose those candidates who are most sensitive to social issues" (p. 19). In this period Don Milani was still a convinced anti-communist, despite esteeming and respecting many communists. This position needs to be understood within the specific historical period: until 1953 Stalin was in power in the USSR. Rather than distancing itself, the Italian communist party adopted a Stalinist-type hierarchical structure. In the United States Truman had drawn up a containment strategy against communism for which the Marshall Plan was an important stronghold. Don Milani's position, however, was clarified during the events that followed. Another "incident" of notable proportions was to be decisive. In July 1952 a priest came to San Donato from Prato to give a sermon. The next day he wrote to his mother: "You must have had a sixth sense when you asked me if I had argued. Yesterday I had an argument that might be decisive. With a priest from Prato who came to preach. I have a feeling that my ecclesiastical career is precipitating."

What had happened exactly? The visiting preacher badly hurt Don Milani's sensibility, denying forgiveness to some of his parishioners during confession. In his reply San Donato's chaplain referred specifically to Giordano. Don Milani recounts the episode:

> That very day I had to run to someone who was ill. Giordano was looking for me and couldn't find me. He saw the good father who I had praised.…After all, he was Christian enough to ask for forgiveness without having to look the Priest in the face. He went to confess.…That evening I saw him and a single glance was enough. He called me aside: *the father asked me about the party. I told him yes. He said he couldn't absolve me unless I tore up my membership card; so?* How much I suffered that evening thanks to that clumsy hand that had devastated my patient and delicate work. I've been bringing him up for four years now with the delicacy of a mother's body that protects her child. That's it, yes, it was like speeding up a birth. Sometimes it's a crime, Father. Sometimes it's necessary, but let the patient's doctor decide, not you who are an outsider, clumsy, incautious, fumbling blindly in another man's garden, transplanting plants that you haven't planted, that you don't know and that you could easily destroy. You know what I did that evening? I was forced to say something that I wish hadn't been necessary, because it wasn't true. I put him at peace, I didn't ask him to do anything to that piece of red card. I told him that the Church decree referred metaphorically to the membership card of his inner self…and I didn't dare raise my eyes to his (Milani, 1957, pp. 272–273).

After the episode in confession, the same priest attacked those men (the communists) in his sermon and Don Milani had Giordano himself next to him:

> You thundered from the pulpit: those men! For you those men were tusked monsters. For Giordano those men represented the pained smile of his dear father, the black faces of his companions in the assembly plant, words of equality, houses for all, work for all, good things mixed up with so many bad things, but good things all the same. And from the pulpit you insisted on kicking him out of church! I felt utterly close to him and totally estranged from you. I felt as if I'd been thrown out of church too and I suffered because I was certain that in the church of Christ the carpenter it was more right for Giordano to be there than for us (Milani, 1957, p. 273).

According to Don Milani the priest from Prato had risked destroying years of work. The public reply was not long in coming in the form of a long letter published in the pages of "Vita Cristiana" and reissued in *Pastoral Experiences*. This episode brought Don Lorenzo to the definitive conclusion that his fate at San Donato was sealed and, even though he hoped in his heart to stay, often speaking about it in his many letters, at times with extreme self-irony, his only fear was that of being condemned for reasons of faith.

After several small yet more or less decisive episodes due to his imprudence, his lack of diplomacy, and his habit of always saying what he thought, Don Milani had added yet more detractors to his rank of enemies. In 1953, with new general elections imminent, he was summoned by the Florentine Curia. On April 25, 1953, Cardinal Dalla Costa and the General Vicar of the Florentine archdiocese, Monsignor Mario Tirapani, were waiting for him. The General Vicar was one of his main detractors and the same who used to make him leave the class when he was still a seminarian because of his criticisms and questions. What's more, as general vicar, he was responsible for the transfer of young priests. On this occasion Tirapani levelled an incredible series of accusations against him, the result of whisperings, slander, backbiting, and aversion. He was accused among other things of favoring the left, not displaying the cross and not speaking of religion in his Popular School, confusing the people with overly refined argument, and causing immense damage to his people (even though it could not be explained how). This time Don Lorenzo was shocked. Once back at the vicarage he wrote a memo to send to Cardinal Dalla Costa along with a typescript of all imaginable data on the social, cultural, economic, and religious conditions of San Donato (this document was to constitute the initial nucleus of *Pastoral Experiences*). Today's documentation is limited to details of the memo, and we do not know with any certainty whether either the memo or the typescript were ever actually sent.

In the 1953 elections he made a further step forward: he invited the Catholics, and no one else, to vote for the best DC candidates (the union leaders) as an act of faith and obedience.

This was followed by other minor episodes, such as his intervention following the mass dismissals in the Doccia ceramics factories. Although he supported the need for a collection in their favor, he intervened publicly during a conference to point out that the offerings would never be enough as long as employers were allowed to freely dismiss their workers. This intervention cost him the manifest opposition of the communists and the right-wing Christian Democrats.

On November 7, 1954, when his transfer was already common news, a report from the Prefect of Florence arrived at the Curia (Allievi di San Donato, Lagomarsini, 2008, p. 80): "discontent reigns among the majority of the population at Calenzano, threatening to transform itself into manifestations of hostility towards the Curia of Florence due to the imminent transfer of the chaplain Don Lorenzo Milani once Albano, priest in charge of the parish of San Donato a Calenzano, following the death of the previous priest in charge."

It was Don Milani himself who did not want to be defended. The only intervention he allowed was that of the parish priest's brother when he was accused of having taken advantage of Don Pugi's old age to deceive him:

The brother of the priest in charge will go to the Curia today to express his appreciation for what I did for him, he will make it known that the priest in charge was not soft in the head and that I neither disobeyed nor deceived him. This is the only intervention that I have allowed in my defence, and indeed asked for because the vulgarity of opposing the priest in charge hurts me.…I plead you not to do anything either. I haven't written to Don Bensi or to Meucci, nor have I been to Florence and if possible I will try to avoid going there. You must understand that a San Donato scandal means nothing to me today and tomorrow it would bring nothing but continuous internal torment for me and external argument with the priests.…I have explained everything to the children and the widows and I am sure that they have understood and that none of them will try anything. That way the new priest will have an easier job and the last thing I will have taught the children will have been religious and coherent with everything else that I have done and that I have asked them to learn in their own interior life (Milani, 1997, pp. 113–116).

Some did try to intervene but the Cardinal's reception was short and cold. Don Milani would not accept any of the compromises that seemed possible and was thus sent, on Tirapani's decision, to Barbiana, a tiny parish on Mount Giovi. The earlier idea was to have a priest sent there to officiate Mass every Sunday. As is often the case, however, the attempt to reduce the priest to silence had the opposite effect. Paradoxically, it was from that isolated church with no road leading up to it that Don Milani's message and work were amplified in a way that would have been impossible to predict.

The Barbiana School: The Beginnings

"You don't measure the greatness of a life by the greatness of the place where it is lived but by other things altogether. And neither do you measure the possibility of doing good by the number of parishioners you have. You know that I need not go looking for anyone, they are the ones who come looking for me and I never have a free minute. Here the school is going full sail."—Letter to his mother dated December 28, 1954; Milani, 1997, pp. 123–124

"I wouldn't lift a finger in favour of the state school today where instead of freedom of ideas, conformism and corruption reign, and if we were to talk about what the state school should be like instead of what it is today then I wouldn't speak about the priests' schools as many of them are today but only about what a few of them are like or, better still, what they should be like.…The selective school system has reached the goal of the middle classes: making working class children hate school."—*I Care Again*

"You are the ones who say that children hate school. You haven't asked us farmers even though there are one billion nine hundred of us."—*Letter to a Teacher*

After the death of the priest Daniele Pugi, Don Milani was sent as prior to Sant'Andrea di Barbiana, at 475 meters above sea level, in the Mugello Mountains, on the north-facing side of Mount Giovi. This was a poor, abandoned land of chestnuts, mushrooms, and blackberries that was unsuitable for agriculture. Barbiana was unequipped with even the most basic services: "There were no pylons for electric light, nor the public telephone's yellow symbol on the vicarage wall, nor was there a road. The only road stopped a few kilometres further down. You went up to the church by way of a sheep track through the woods that had been made by passing flocks and sledges."[28]

Don Milani arrived in Barbiana in the rain on December 6, 1954. There was no light, no road, and no water. A handful of families lived scattered over the mountains in the parish that had once been destined to close. Don Milani didn't come alone. Eda and Giulia Pelagatti, who had once looked after Don Pugi and then Don Milani at San Donato, decided to follow Don Milani to Barbiana on the death of the priest in charge. The ascent to the vicarage in the pouring rain, arm in arm with "Grandma" (as he would call Giulia Pelagatti), had a strong effect on him. As soon as he got to Barbiana he went into the church and cried. The old prior left a few days after with his family. The vicarage and the place as a whole were in terrible condition. It was impossible to get there in the removal van and the few pieces of furniture that weren't already damaged or chipped got broken, covered in mud, and ruined in the move because of the rain. Don Milani set to work, helped by the children who lived there. On Sundays the parishioners from San Donato came up in turn to visit and helped him cut, clean, paint, clear, and mend. It wasn't long before he started work on a road with the help of the children. Between one manual job and another he immediately set up the evening school as he had already promised to the young people from Barbiana who had come to visit him at San Donato before the move.

One of the first things Don Milani did was to buy a place for himself in the small cemetery where he is buried today in his vestments and his mountain shoes. Even more so than at San Donato, the school for the working-class mountain people was to become the center of his mission and his life. It needed no promotion as this letter to Don Bensi, his spiritual father, testified just 23 days after his arrival at Barbiana (the letter is dated December 29): "I didn't waste any time publicizing the school. As soon as I mentioned it to someone I immediately found the school full of young lads. All working class without exception and from this evening there are even going to be a few from the neighbouring parishes. Everyone comes from afar because the church is completely isolated" (Milani, 2007, p. 49).

Optimistic, ironic, and hard-working, Don Milani wrote to convince himself and others of his immediate love of the place; as if he had always lived there; as if he had always been accustomed to its discomforts; as if, deep down, part of him had always been a mountain man. The events of his transfer had clearly weighed on him, even though he rarely mentioned them, as transpires from this letter to his mother: "I can't believe you want me to think of myself as just passing through or being on holiday. Don Bensi and Meucci have written me letters just like yours. It's obvious that none of you realize what San Donato meant to me. Otherwise you wouldn't be so cruel as to talk to me about the next amputation in the very days when I am still convalescing, only alive thanks to a miracle of grace. Why do you talk about tomorrow? Aren't today's worries enough for you? And there's no need to think that my wings have been clipped just because I'm up here" (Milani, 1997, p. 123).

The pain of the amputation was absorbed by the proximity of San Donato, whose parishioners never missed a chance to visit and express their affection for him, showering him with attentions and small gifts that the misery of the times allowed, and above all by the school:

> I've had to make toys and puppets for the school to replace all those things we did at San Donato with the projector. Today I made a huge poster with the score of the VII symphony[29] that I'm waiting for Elena to bring me on Sunday. I've had to make do with two classrooms. The lower level class is in my study and the older children take it in turns to lead it. When I have guests from San Donato they take the class....At San Donato I never had so much fun teaching as I do here. Everything's new, everything's accepted, everything fascinates them (Milani, 1997, p. 129).

In the early stages the Barbiana school copied the structure of San Donato. It was open to adult students in the evenings, except when the weather was bad and the farmers stopped their work in the mountains. Later it acquired the specificity of the Barbiana experience, open all day to pupils who were more or less the right age for obligatory schooling. Initially, when the school was only open in the evenings and sometimes in the afternoons to help the children from the elementary school at Padulivo, he had time to think, to ski, and in the winter months especially when visits were few and far between, to work on *Pastoral Experiences,* which was to come out in 1958.

The numerous letters and recounts of the time let us imagine an all-rounder who was unbending and harsh but also humane, gentle, and incredibly delicate, capable of smiling and encouraging (Fallaci, 1993, pp. 225–231).

The school soon turned into the place that would make it famous all over Italy and beyond: 12 hours a day of lessons for 365 days a year, 366 in leap years. In those years the teaching of the children entrusted to him became the true objective of his work as a priest. He was no longer concerned solely with their instruction as it was understood at the time. He broadened his horizons, devoting large amounts of time to the learning of languages, for example, using records and recordings (a method already tried out at San Donato). He encouraged the children's independence by taking them to Florence, first himself, then with a friend, and lastly alone. He used his contacts so that they could travel abroad, even when they were just 15 years old and barely adult, before they had to start work and would no longer have time to do anything else. "A trip abroad was like the end of school exam for the prior's pupils" (Fallaci, 1993, p. 363). Don Milani managed to convince the parents about this as many of the children had seen the sea for the first time in 1955 thanks to a trip that he himself had organized. He assured them that he would go and get their children himself if there were any problems and he prepared them at length with extreme care. As Franco Gesualdi and Neera Fallaci explain: "He didn't suddenly hurl us abroad from the isolated world of Barbiana. The trips abroad marked the end of a long preparatory period. When a boy was shy, Don Lorenzo would start taking him to Florence with him, then he would send him with another boy and then he would send him on his own to do jobs and go round offices for him. Before letting us go abroad we would do hours of lessons on train timetables. He taught us how to read timetables, how to change trains, how to plan out an itinerary" (Fallaci, 1993, p. 364). Before they left he would also write tens of letters to his acquaintances, friends, friends of relatives, and relatives and acquaintances of friends. He would write to them all in their languages to ensure that the children would have a network to protect them. He would write to all of the children abroad and it was his habit to read the letters aloud in class. When his illness got worse and his "sons and daughters" around the world were too many to write to separately he thought up the idea of the circular letter. The first one was titled *Circular Letter from the Republic of Barbiana to All of Its Diplomatic Representatives Abroad. Their Offices.*

Furthermore, from 1959 he began "hosting young foreign people at Barbiana so that his pupils could practice conversation in French, English or German. The first in the series was Michel: a pupil of a French priest who ran a school in a mountain parish just like Don Milani" (Fallaci, 1993, pp. 361–362). "Lots of languages badly" Don Milani would say "rather than one well," and it is through affirmations such as these that it is possible to comprehend Don Milani's concept of culture and education. Culture was at the service of the children and not the opposite; education was a tool to improve oneself and one's existence, rather than to chase up a qualification or pay homage to grammar. He favored autonomous reading (thanks to the donations of books that began arriving with some regularity); even when he doubted the appropriateness of certain books (with obvious severity) he felt that for children of that age, even when in doubt, it was still better to read.

Changes to the Italian School System in the Mid-1950s

In 1955 the minister Giuseppe Ermini issued new programs for general education[30] that were to mark the height of the Catholic interpretation of the school.[31] The child was seen to be a kind of primitive being, totally dominated by the imagination, intuition, and feeling—with mostly negative connotations. It was thus necessary to start from general intuitions to then proceed to reasoning, theorizing, and considered thought. The teaching of the language focused on proper speaking. These programs "while trying to find an equilibrium between Deweyan activism and Catholic personalism, giving some space to the free initiative of the teacher, actually revealed hints of Catholic fundamentalism in the absolute pre-eminence given to religious education. These signs, alongside the concluding references to moral and religious values, were recognizable even in the most significant part of the Introduction, where, on the trail of Decrolian and Deweyan activism[32] the teacher's attention was called to focus upon the child's environment: In the psychology of the child intuition of the whole comes before the analytical recognition of its parts. The task of the school is to facilitate this natural process, beginning with the first global intuitions and then gradually articulating them within a considered discourse.…On the other hand, an awareness of the fundamental characteristics of the infantile soul places the school on a line of natural continuity with what the child has already learned, understood and felt within his family circle, his natural social environment, and within the other educational institutions that he has attended. The teacher must not therefore forget that the child is a member of and participates in the life of its surrounding environment in its various forms and in the moral and religious aspiration that animates it" (Corbi and Sarracino, 1999, pp. 80–81).

The most obviously class-based aspect of the program, and probably the most serious regression, can be seen in the attempt (through bureaucratic procedures intended to avoid parliamentary debate on this point) to set up a three-year post-elementary school for those children who would not have gone beyond primary education (the children of the less-well-off classes). This solution was a remedy for obligatory schooling up to 13 years of age, dictated by the constitution, and established an inferior level of schooling that would only be changed in 1962 with the unified middle school system. The heavy-handed rhetoric was intended to impede any form of accelerated social transformation. Justifications for the program did not even attempt to disguise the concept that these children were equipped with inferior cognitive abilities; on the contrary, it was believed that the program was to "favour the discovery of the pupil's interests and abilities in manual and practical activities; help him find his place in the social and economic context." It is clear how the rationale put forward opposed mind and hand, theory and practice, while the extremely modest syllabus kept the children from poorer classes from learning anything but the bare cultural basics, confirmed by the necessity that transpires in the preliminary indications, to create "a climate of voluntary industriousness that liberates them from the risk of having to study things that are foreign to their interests or submit themselves to endeavours that they do not understand the purpose of." Don Milani's work clearly developed in complete contrast to what was outlined by the State, not just because of the intrinsic value attributed to every pupil and the emancipatory value accredited to the development of the person through school life but also because of an educational vision that was much more modern than the programs and indications issued in those years. It is only through our understanding of how state schooling in those years wanted to maintain the social order and not only reproduce inequality but find meanings and justifications to support it that we can understand the disruptive effect of Milani's work in this period. These programs were to remain valid until 1984 (with the only exception of the unified middle school system that proceeded from elementary school), 30 years in which Italian society was to change radically. Nevertheless it would be mistaken to think that the Milani experience was completely isolated. In the same years a movement known as the MCE (Cooperative Education Movement) grew up following the work of Celestin Freinet who placed the child at the center of the entire educational process; the child's world, language, freedom, and creative expression became fundamental values. Teaching was contextualized locally and posed social questions. Well-known exponents of the movement included teachers such as Mario Lodi, Gianni Rodari, Bruno Ciari, and Giuseppe Tamagnini (founder of the movement).

The government adopted the same line in *Directions for Educational Activity in Nursery Schooling* in 1958, which, as with elementary schools, marked a retrograde step with regard to previous policy.

Pastoral Experiences: A Book Withdrawn from Publication

In April 1958 after infinite rereadings, rewritings, and unbelievable fault finding, the volume *Pastoral Experiences* was finally printed, together with a long and meditated preface by Archbishop of Camerino Mons. D'Avack and regular priming.[33] The book focuses on his work at San Donato and is an exceptional sociological document on the San Donato of the time. Don Milani patiently classifies living conditions (from the number of beds to the presence/absence of electric lighting and running water), forms of transport, the number of people who went to Mass and received communion, the positions occupied in church, the number of children and their level of education, and everything that one could possible imagine about life at the time, in an attempt to understand his community better and respond to his own questions regarding the secularization of those people. Lorenzo Milani's sensitivity as a "convert" led him to notice the mechanical religious practice of his parishioners—their participation in rituals they often barely understood. His indefatigable curiosity and desire to express himself and understand others are well documented in this work. An enormous mass of data was collected "drawing from the town council and parish archives. The majority was collected directly" (Fallaci, 1993, p. 239).

Barbiana is also mentioned, Milani referring to himself as if he was a different person from San Donato's chaplain: a colleague, brother and correspondent with whom he had much in common. Davide Maria Turoldo, another "awkward" personality in those years, had offered to publish the book with the Servi di Maria publishing house that he was part of. In a letter to the magistrate Meucci, one of his dearest friends, Don Milani wrote:

> You say that a book is an act of intelligence and therefore secondary, meaning that it can be written down without too much thought. On the contrary, I think at length about it and measure the value of the words I write down because I know how much I paid for my words and actions at San Donato and I imagine how much I will have to pay for these. If they are going to cost me so much, I want at least to be sure that I have paid the price for a proportionately serious work. On this point I want you to know that when I say I want to keep on working on the book, I'm not in the least interested, as you claim, in its aesthetic perfection, I just want to rethink the things I say, to be sure that's what I really think and to be sure that's the right way of thinking, etc. (Milani, 2007, p. 91).

Mons. D'Avack's preface, which Milani beseeched him to write through Meucci (so that he would intercede with La Pira on his behalf) and Don Bensi, had a specific motivation: "A priest of 110 souls in a diocese that has tens of much larger parishes with no priests is not a very good sign and doesn't help inspire faith neither in a pupil, a penitent, a parishioner nor a reader. A few words from a bishop would do me the world of good in every way so if you and La Pira can do anything to help me obtain them I pray you to do so" (Milani, 2007, p. 92).

Initial reactions were positive and the book received a series of quite enthusiastic reviews. Don Primo Mazzolari, another important figure at the time, was interested. Monsignor Facibeni devoted an entire edition of his paper, "Il Focolare," to the prior and his book but died the day after having expressed his intention to review it personally to a colleague, leaving the volume open on his desk at page 83, where he had underlined the following lines: "the reason lies among other things in the inability of religious figures to grasp the situation and language of our peoples" (Milani, 1957, p. 83). The text went on to say, "this book is a testimony to the difficulty of a priest in understanding the environment within which he has been living for years."

It was not long, however, before the discussion around the book became more threatening, starting with a negative review by the *Settimana del Clero*, quickly followed by another in *La Civiltà Cattolica*, until by order of the Holy Office, the book disappeared from circulation, due to its "unsuitability." After having held up the book as an example, the *Osservatore Romano*, the Holy See's official paper, tried to justify the regular priming, putting it down to a series of misunderstandings and achieving the double aim of "demonizing" Don Milani and exonerating the Diocesan authorities.

Letters of the time reveal Don Milani's preoccupation with the book's consequences for those who had allowed it to be published rather than for himself. Just as everything seemed to have calmed down, partly as a result of Pope Pius XII's death on October 9, 1958, which distracted everybody's attention, the events reached a conclusion. On December 20, 1958, the *Osservatore Romano* published an unsigned article at the end of the paper: "The Supreme Holy Congregation of the Holy Office has ordered the book *Pastoral Experiences* by Don Milani to be withdrawn from publication and has furthermore forbidden any reprinting or translations. This measure is undoubtedly meant to be a serious warning to the children of the Church and in particular to its Priests, so as not to be seduced by daring and dangerous novelties that threaten to insinuate themselves into the souls of those less prepared for the serious and demanding task of the apostle in the social field." It had clearly not been possible to find even the slightest reason for an attack on doctrinal lines, and so the Holy Office could not blame the book for heresy (which would have been an immense pain for the prior), but could only judge it as "inappropriate," claiming the unusual right to withdraw the book from publication and forbidding its reprint or translation.

Naturally, the attention that followed was both well intentioned and malicious. The book had already been much talked about and after the Holy Office's announcement and the order to withdraw it from publication, it was talked about even more, even by those who had not read it. The days following the publication of the Holy Office's decree were difficult, yet typically of Don Lorenzo, while suffering badly (as is obvious from some of his expressions and confidences), he managed to draw a ferocious irony from what had happened; see the letter written to his mother on Christmas Day of 1958 (five days after the *Osservatore Romano*'s announcement):

> I am as busy as a minister surrounded and ensnared on all sides by flashes and stenographers. The day before yesterday the Tribune (not the illustrated tribune) of Milan; yesterday the Vie Nuove and the Unità da Roma; today Anna Maria Ortese from Rome, another famous socialist writer (the sea hasn't touched Naples). At the same time other journalists have attacked San Donato, interrogating people from house to house. Yesterday the first bus came and tomorrow the second is coming. In short, a stressful life and I really think I'm going to have to ask for a transfer to another smaller parish.... The post arrives at a rate of 20 letters a day, among which some from brothers and some that are so sadistically malicious as to make me want to hand them over for publication to some of these journalists. So far I have resisted the temptation (Milani, 1997, pp. 181–182).

His complete absorption in the school, in the letters and visits that expressed esteem, and in the daily problems posed by his children made this historical event quickly fade into the background: in the letters written just a couple of months later there was only the occasional biting comment.

The Late Period

In 1960 Don Milani first became aware of the symptoms of an illness that would lead him to his death within seven years, Hodgkin's disease or malign lymphogranulomatosis (an unusual form of leukemia). He paid relatively little attention to it and was often ironic about it. In 1961 in a letter to his mother he made a passing reference to two sleepless nights because of terrible pains, but then everything seemed to get back to normal.

His final years of work at Barbiana brought him countless satisfaction both from "his" children and from his participation in considerably important public events.

After the events surrounding his first book hit the headlines, Don Milani became a public figure and everything he did that wasn't lost in the secret isolation of Barbiana was news.

In its initial phase the Barbiana school was an after-school club that didn't simply complement the Padulivo Elementary School where the Barbiana children received their primary education but redressed the low level of education guaranteed by the school's "multi-classes."

> For the whole of the winter they spend the morning with their teacher and the afternoon at school with me and in their spare time they work. In the summer they work from dawn

> until noon and in the afternoon they are at school with me until it gets dark. On Sundays they come to school in the morning and afternoon, the only interruption being for Mass and Vespers. They never have holidays, they never play. Not because I don't let them, but mostly because I don't mention it and so it doesn't even occur to them that they might have earned a day's holiday. What for? Where would they go? Life doesn't reserve any other expectations for them except work and school. Each serves as a break from the other.…They are capable of being in school eight or nine hours a day without blinking an eyelid; no complaints, no insistence on rights, they are grateful and happy out of the joy of learning (Milani, 1957, p. 159, 160).

Between 1956 and 1957 two orphaned brothers from Puglia came and lived at the vicarage with Don Milani, Michele and Francuccio Gesualdi. In the same period the vocational school opened with six pupils. In Italy in that period the unified middle school system still did not exist; it was to be established later. With his vocational school Don Milani managed to convince some families not to leave the mountains, despite the fact that some of the fathers worked as far away as Vicchio. From the beginning the school was open 365 days a year, 366 in a leap year, as the prior himself loved to point out.

In these years Don Milani clarified his pedagogical concept, which centered on the development of the person, determination, independence, and will power, as can clearly be seen from many of the letters written during those years. In 1956, for example, he wrote to a young man from San Donato who had failed his driving test three times because of his shyness:

> I was really upset to hear about you failing your test. I really wasn't expecting this. I'm glad to see that you got it right with Caterina [a girl who is seriously ill]. Now I expect you to take another step forward. What happened with Caterina will help you forget about the incident of the driving test. And thinking about me, about you, about your future and how hard it will be to start all over again and the complications that the new driving regulations will create, all these things must help you take your test and try again before your provisional license runs out. Whatever it takes. The man who gives up in the face of the smallest and most ordinary of life's adversities can't go on living, he'll be a wretch his whole life, he won't find a wife or a job and nor will he be able to win over his passions and his vices. There was once a famous man (I can't remember his name) who was in prison and very disheartened. He saw a spider who was trying to climb up a smooth wall and kept on falling back down and every time he fell he tried again. I don't remember if the spider ever got up the wall but I remember that that man had the courage to start all over again. And you will be like him otherwise you'll be half a man, a coward.

His words for everyone, endless letters, conversations, grumbling, encouragements, pep talks, gestures of love, and his incredible ability to intuitively understand how and when to intervene with his pupils and ex-pupils were all at the center of Don Milani's pedagogy. The motivation and desire for autonomy and development were fundamental for him, alongside the pedagogy of mistakes. One way which Don Milani anticipated modern theories of learning and education was the centrality of activity within the school, whether it was trying to write a collective text (and rewrite, rewrite again, correct, refine, and rewrite again) or learning how to make a door, bend iron, or make an educational toy. When Don Milani opened the vocational school he wasn't capable of guiding his pupils in carpentry or mechanics and so, despite their initial resistance, he brought in two craftsmen from neighboring Vicchio (Giuseppe Cipriani, a 20-year-old carpenter, and Bruno Cantini, an ironmonger and mechanic). He said to Bruno Cantini, "You get them to weld something and then you show them where they went wrong and that way they learn. This way they understand better because they learn through their mistakes, they understand how they got things wrong and why" (Sessi, 2008, p. 135).

The first six pupils succeeded in obtaining their diploma studying with Don Lorenzo and the two craftsmen involved, but the prior naturally took advantage of every single person who came to visit him, immediately setting them up to converse, teach, and discuss with his pupils.[34] As the school's reputation spread Don Milani began to realize that he could not do it all on his own, and he began to organize things so that the older children taught the younger ones. The presence of Professor Ammannati and Professor Adele Corradi[35] (who asked for a transfer to be closer to the Barbiana school) provided significant support to the school.

Despite his precarious health in later years the prior intensified his work where possible. In 1961 he traveled to Stockholm with some of his pupils and on his return he carried out a series of necessary jobs in the school and church:

> There are exactly 30 children here in the school. The 6 older ones don't seem to want to leave; we didn't even have enough desks and benches for everyone. So we started by making some furniture all in solid mahogany (remember all that mahogany I told you about that Paolo gave us). A small table for the typewriter, a huge table to use in school and for dinner time, two enormous benches, 2 playpens for the babies and a new glass door for the workshop. In Germany we found out about a cheap way of making stained glass and we made two for the church, the third one is the main one for the façade and that one's still being designed (Milani, 1997, p. 202).[36]

They even built a small swimming pool 8 meters long and just 2 meters wide. It wasn't for playing but for teaching those mountain folk who were scared of water how to swim.

In 1963 the journalist and friend Giorgio Pecorini, who had visited Milani to review *Pastoral Experiences,* came to Barbiana bringing with him Mario Lodi.

Mario Lodi was one of the protagonists of the Cooperative Education Movement, which followed in the footsteps of Freinet in trying to develop his methods in Italy with the active involvement of children, the positive evaluation of their experiences and skills, and their participation as protagonists in their own learning process. Mario Lodi and Lorenzo Milani agreed to organize an exchange of letters between the children from their two schools. At Barbiana they worked indefatigably and continuously for nine days on their letter to the children of Vho, and on November 1, 1963, the famous letter "Why I Go to School"[37] was posted. The letter is harmonious and rich in meaning. The Barbiana school is described in seven points: "if our school wasn't here to stop our parents from moving, Barbiana would be a desert" (Milani, 2007, p. 211):

> Ours is a private school situated in two of the rooms in the vicarage plus another two that we use as workshops. In the winter it's a bit tight but from April to October we do our lessons outside and so there's no lack of space! Now there are 29 of us. 3 girls and 26 boys. Only nine pupils come from families who live in the parish of Barbiana. The other five live with other families because their own families live too far away. The other 15 are from other parishes and go home every day, some on foot, some by bicycle, some by scooter. Some of them come from very far away, like Luciano who has to walk through the wood for almost two hours there and back again. The youngest of us is 11 and the oldest 18….Our timetable is from 8 in the morning to 7.30 in the evening and we have a short break for lunch….We have 23 teachers! Because each one of us teaches the ones who are younger than us, except for the youngest (pp. 211–212).

The letter describes why they (and their parents) had chosen to enroll at the school: "we didn't all come for the same reasons….Nobody thought of getting a diploma so as to earn more money or work less hard in the future. The idea didn't occur to us spontaneously and if it did occur to some of us, it was only because we were influenced by our parents" (p. 213); and why they still came to school at the moment of writing the letter,

> Slowly we realized that this is a special school: there are no marks, no reports and no risk of failing or having to repeat a year. With all the hours and days we are at school, exams are easy so we can get through the whole year without having to think about them too much. We don't ignore them completely though, because we want to make our parents happy with that piece of paper that they hold in such admiration, otherwise they wouldn't let us come any more….This deep, rich school where nobody feels afraid made all of us want to keep coming after just a few days. And that's not all: after a few months each of us was fascinated by knowledge in itself. But we still had one discovery to make: loving knowledge can be selfish too. The prior showed us a higher ideal: to look for knowledge so as to use it for serving others; for example, dedicating our adult lives to teaching or politics or the trade unions or the apostolic life or other such things (p. 214).

The letter then goes on to reflect on the gap between intention and action ("it's easier said than done"): "All of us would like to live today and for the rest of our lives in the light of these ideals. But under pressure from our parents, the middle class world and a pinch of our own selfishness, we are all continuously tempted to fall back into only thinking of ourselves" (p. 215); it then elaborates on the issue of parental pressure and pressure from the wider world, concluding with reference to parents: "this school has helped us to defend ourselves, yet our poor parents haven't had this or any other kind of schooling."

This is an extraordinary account worth reading in its entirety to fully understand the workings and atmosphere of the Barbiana School. The letters are also testimony to the dialogue between two experiences that are way ahead of their times and to Don Milani's informal integration within the educational debate of the time.

Don Milani's final years were marked by new controversy that was to make him even more widely known to a wider audience. On Sunday, February 14, 1965, Professor Ammannati arrived in Barbiana with some young people from Calenzano as often happened on Sundays, and they showed the prior some clippings from a newspaper article that had appeared two days earlier. The clippings were read aloud after mass. At the Military Institute of Florence some army chaplains on leave had voted an item at the end of their meeting: "On the anniversary of the conciliation between the Church and the Italian State the army chaplains on leave in Tuscany came together yesterday at the Institute for the Holy Family in via Lorenzo il Magnifico. They paid reverent and brotherly tribute to all those fallen in battle for Italy, praying in the name of God for an end, finally, to every discrimination, every one-sided division in the name of every soldier on every military front and in every uniform who has died, sacrificing himself for the sacred of ideal of Homeland. They consider 'conscientious objection' to be an insult to the homeland and to those fallen in battle, foreign to the Christian commandment of love and an expression of cowardice" (*La Nazione* newspaper, February 12, 1965). The prior had never addressed the issue of conscientious objection, for which the well-known Piarist, Father Balducci, had been condemned to eight months of imprisonment (he had defended Giuseppe Gozzini, who as a Catholic had refused to do his military service). However, in the presence of his pupils Don Milani could not exempt himself from answering, as he writes in his *Letter to the Judiciary*:

> Now, I was sitting in front of my children in my double role as teacher and priest and they were looking at me, indignant and passionate. A priest who insults a prisoner is always wrong, even more so if he who has been insulted is imprisoned for his ideals. There was no need to tell my children these things, they had already understood them for themselves, and they had also realized that I was committed to giving them one of life's lessons (Milani, 1965, p. 43).

Lorenzo Milani could not back down. One might imagine him already very ill, embittered by previous conflicts, intent on getting the most out of his educational experience. Knowing the end was in sight he would have wanted to escape this new controversy, and yet he believed it was not right. It was found out later that there were 20 chaplains on leave present at the meeting and at least 100 missing, and yet he felt it his duty to respond. The news had appeared in the newspaper *La Nazione* so Don Milani felt he should send a public reply and sent off his letter to all the newspapers and all the priests in Florence. As he was to explain in the first half of his letter, he doesn't refer to the New Testament because "it's too easy to demonstrate that Jesus was against violence and didn't accept legitimate defence even for himself. I will refer to the Constitution." The letter is a civil lesson of immense value that starts from the idea of conscientious objection and ends with a discussion on the concept of obedience.

> Tell us exactly what you have taught these soldiers. Obedience at all costs? And what if orders include civilian bombardment, retaliation against a defenceless village, the summary execution of partisans, the use of atomic weapons, bacteriological weapons, chemical weapons, torture, the execution of hostages, summary trials for straightforward suspects, decimation…, an obviously aggressive war, the repression of popular demonstrations? And yet these and many others are the daily bread of every war. When they have gone on right in front of you, you have either lied or kept quiet. Or do you want us to believe that every time it's happened you've always told the truth to your superiors risking prison or death? If you're still alive and have graduated then it means you've never objected to anything (p. 21).

He clearly retraces an analysis of conscientious objection in his text (for which you could go to prison in Italy at the time) with reference to international law and by pointing out how to avoid particular stereotypes: "In many civil countries (more civil than ours in this case) the law honours them by allowing them to serve their Country in another way. They ask to sacrifice themselves for their country more than others, not less. It's not their fault if in Italy they have no other choice than to fade away in prison." In his letter Don Milani runs through the history of Italy and enjoys demonstrating the absurd futility and savagery of the wars that have animated the 100-year history of Italian unity. The letter also attacks the idea of the Homeland, inherited by fascism, and thus concludes:

> We respect suffering and death, but in front of the young that are looking at us let's not create any dangerous confusion about the difference between good and evil, truth and error, the death of an aggressor and the death of his victim. If you wish, we can say: let us pray for the unhappy ones who have been poisoned against their will by the propaganda of hate and have sacrificed themselves for the single misunderstood ideal of the Homeland, treading on every other noble human ideal without even noticing (Milani, 1965, p. 28).

In these heated times everything happened quickly. At first the letter wasn't published by the papers, but on March 6 *Rinascita*, the Communist Party journal edited by Luca Pavolini, issued it in its full-length version. Not long after that a group of ex-soldiers made a formal written report against Don Milani, *Rinascita*, and its editor. Barbiana was flooded with obscene and offensive letters full of fascist threats, swastikas, and gallows.[38] On March 31 the Vicchio town council organized a meeting on the religious, juridical, cultural, and political aspects of conscientious objection. Don Milani was guest of honor. At the last minute the Florentine Curia intervened to stop all priests (and therefore the prior himself) from participating. As a result everyone interpreted Don Milani's opinions as they deemed fit and although he was sorry he'd had to leave them without an answer, although he felt embittered yet again that no official voice from the Church had been raised in his defense, he nevertheless had to keep quiet and bite his tongue in as much as Cardinal Florit had threatened him with *divine suspension* (suspension from his functions as a priest) unless he agreed to submit every one of his pieces before making them public in any way. In the meantime, the report against him took its course and in July he received a mandate to appear in court on October 30, 1965. He refused to nominate a lawyer for the hearing and one was assigned to him. He was asked not to intervene, but he explained that for ethical reasons he could not guarantee he would remain silent. His illness' advancement would certainly not have allowed him to be present in Rome where the hearing was to be held, so he used the months that separated him from the hearing to set down the extremely well-known *Letter to the Judges* (now published together with *Letter to the Army Chaplains* in *Obedience Is No Longer a Virtue*). It is a worthy document of great civil interest that underlines some important principles and reconfirms Lorenzo Milani's educational thought. He writes to the judges:

> I had to teach them how a citizen should react to injustice. How he has freedom of speech and freedom of press. How a Christian should react to a priest or even a bishop who errs. How everyone should feel responsible for everything. On a wall in our school we have written the words **I Care**. It is the untranslated motto of the best young Americans. I care: it's important to me. It's the exact opposite of the fascist motto: "I couldn't care less" (Milani, 2007, p. 272).

The hearing ended on February 15, 1966. The public prosecutor asked the court to pass a sentence of eight months' imprisonment, but the court issued a verdict of absolute acquittal. In the appeal hearing the sentence was overturned but it was October 28, 1967, and Lorenzo Milani had already passed away, four months earlier.

In the last months of his life Lorenzo Milani was embittered by a letter dated January 25, 1966, from Cardinal Florit who defined him as "by nature absolutist,…an oppressor of souls more than a Father," filling his letter with other accusations based little on fact and mostly on slander. He enclosed 300 thousand lira in his letter, knowing that Don Milani was seriously ill, but the letter had a profound effect on the prior, who was debilitated and bedridden. He instituted the "continental block," that is, an absolute ban on anyone with a qualification higher than the middle school diploma from coming to visit, apart from named exceptions. The Cardinal's fleeting interest, however, did not stop, he even went to see him at his bedside in March 1966, an "agonizing hour" as Florit himself was to define it. Don Milani wrote to his mother: "The meeting with the Cardinal was extraordinarily reassuring. His malice is so evident, his unsuppressed hate and pride make one automatically feel in the right, overwhelmed with sanctity and reason."

Barbiana stopped accepting new pupils, the end was near, everybody was aware of it even though they talked about it rarely: "I'm dismantling the school," he wrote to Mrs. Lovato in March 1966.

> I've sent the oldest ones to work and I'm not taking any new pupils. There are still about ten kids who I'm teaching in my room. Or when I'm tired they do their lessons in the room next door and then my educational activity consists in the odd shout to keep them quiet. I've got leukemia and I don't want to die stupidly while I'm still on the cutting edge with immature kids who are half educated and half not. So for the last year I've been organizing a modest and restful decline (Milani, 2007, p. 318).

However, in a letter to Edoardo, one of the boys who had found work in England after going there to learn the language, he announced: "We're working at a great letter, like the one to the judiciary. This one's against teachers." The occasion presented itself after the terrible exam results of three boys from Barbiana who were studying to become teachers: Enrico, Luciano, and Michele. The three failures added to two from the year before. The letter was totally lucid, a collective work by the whole school, and expressed Don Milani's entire educational thought. Schools pass and fail but they don't do so equally: the school is a tool for social conservation, a tool to maintain the existing distance between social classes when it should be used to reduce that gap. Schools don't respect the Constitution because they don't encourage; on the contrary, they impede the full development of every person and the effective participation of all future workers within the social, political, and economic organization of Italy. Written to a teacher (metaphorically the one who failed the Barbiana pupils), it is a high-quality document (as well as being aesthetically important) and a historical analysis of the Italian education system.

With the clarity of reasoning typical of him, supported by data, it is considered by many as one of the key texts on the sociology of the Italian education system. The text is so deeply contemporary that it is still useful to read today—being more than an important historical document and fundamental step in understanding Don Milani's thought. It is not possible to reduce it to a synthesis but needs to be read in full to comprehend its goal, the solid argument and vision that make it a ferocious attack on the state school system of the time.

In March 1967 Don Milani moved to his mother's house in Florence because he had to undergo further radiotherapy. He returned to Barbiana for a brief interlude in April when he burned a large part of his private correspondence.

Lorenzo Milani died on June 26, 1967. Just one month before, in May 1967, *Letter to a Teacher* had come out. Perhaps his most famous work, it is a radical critique of the model that dominated the state school institution of the time—an Italian school system that was brutally selective and capable of distancing and excluding the children of mountain communities, farmers, and workers. In this work, written together with his pupils, Don Milani criticizes the underlying school culture whose objectives are centered purely on scholastic promotion and the possibility of obtaining a qualification. The listlessness and superficial participation that he has observed bring him to comment "this kind of pedagogy should be got rid of" unless it becomes capable of telling us "that all children are different, each historical period is different as is every period of a child's life, the places where they live, their environment, their families" (Milani and Scuola di Barbiana, 1967, p. 119).

Don Milani's school was a fundamental step in the history of education and its institutions. Don Milani's main aim, pursued through the theory of individualization and personalization, is the promotion of educational success for all pupils, whatever context they come from, to allow each of us to consciously exercise our rights of citizenship within society. It is a school that promotes autonomy, critical thinking, and culture as a tool for freeing oneself from oppression, a school that allows each person to increase control over his or her life and his or her choices and to take an interest in the lives of others.

Don Lorenzo was buried at Barbiana, as he had wished.

3

Lorenzo Milani and the School of Barbiana's Pedagogical Approach

> Because there is nothing as unjust as trying to create equality among those who are not equal.
> —School of Barbiana, in Borg, Cardona, and Caruana, 2009, p. 155

Lorenzo Milani has been gaining recognition as a figure who can provide insights for a critical approach to education. He is certainly revered in Southern Europe, especially in his native Italy, for his radical approach to education and schooling in particular. He has gained recognition in the English-speaking world since some of the works he wrote (those concerning his trial and tribulations) and others with which he is strongly associated, such as the *Lettera,* have been translated into English and have been the subject of some insightful discussions. Three years following its publication in Italian in 1967, the *Lettera* was published in English translation by the U.S. publishing house Random House. In Britain, the Open University used the Penguin edition of the English version of the *Lettera* as a text. It was a featured text in a course on Schooling and Society (E 202) that started in 1974.[1] In 1988, the University of Indiana Press published J. T. Burtchaell's *A Just War No Longer Exists. The Teaching and Trial of Don Lorenzo Milani,* which includes translated versions of the *Lettera ai Giudici* (Letter to the Judges), the *Lettera ai Cappellani* (the Letter to the Military Chaplains), and other material related to the accusations levelled at Milani for his advocacy of conscientious objection to military conscription, discussed in detail in the previous chapter. In 1977, ten years after its original publication in Italian, the *Lettera a una Professoressa* was also published in Turkish.

The *Lettera* has also been translated into Spanish and read in Freire's Latin America, albeit clandestinely in those countries that went through fascist dictatorial periods. Daniel Schugurensky, an Argentinean professor at Arizona State University, writes with reference to the *Lettera*: "I remember reading the Spanish version of the book in the early seventies in my secondary school in Argentina. Needless to say, it was not part of the school curriculum. My classmate Carlos Vanney lent it to me during a break with an air of secrecy and a mischievous smile, as if he were passing on to me a forbidden and powerful document that was going to change my understanding of schooling. It did. Gracias Carlos!"[2]

As stated in the Introduction, however, despite his special credentials to feature in the pantheon of leading critical education figures, and as someone whose ideas are worth mining for developing a critical pedagogy, Lorenzo Milani has been given scant attention in the English-speaking world. He is less known than, for instance, Paulo Freire (1921–1997) in critical education circles. It is only recently that he started being considered as a potential international contributor to that area known as critical pedagogy (Borg and Mayo, 2006). This chapter will highlight some of the main elements of Milani's critical approach to education, an approach that is predicated on social justice. As with Freire and other major exponents of critical pedagogy, his pedagogical approach signifies "an option for the oppressed," or, to echo Dolci, *i poveri Cristi* (the poor Christs).

Milani and Other Critical Pedagogues: Any Influence?

It would be anachronistic to suggest that critical pedagogy's internationally most-heralded pedagogue, Paulo Freire, had any influence on Milani given the year when the latter passed away (1967) and despite the striking similarities in some of their pedagogical approaches and their underlying concern for the underprivileged, the oppressed in Freire's language and *I Gianni bocciati* (the failed Giannis) in the language of the *Lettera* written, under Lorenzo's direction, by eight pupils from the School of Barbiana who would each be considered a "Gianni." The name refers to a child who at 14 joined the school after having been flunked several times at Vicchio (S. Gesualdi, 2007, p. x). It is, however, plausible that Paulo Freire would have been exposed to the name and legacy of Don Milani and the School of

Barbiana during the time when he worked in Geneva for the World Council of Churches. It is possible, though we find virtually no references in his widely published work in English, that Freire came across such a legacy during his meetings with Italian workers, trade unionists, and educators both in Geneva and Italy. Milani had already been enjoying considerable influence throughout Italy at the time following the publication of *Esperienze Pastorali* (Pastoral Experiences) and the *Lettera*, the latter in 1967, the year of his death.

'68 and All That!

The *Lettera* was written as a reaction to the fact that two Barbiana students, il Biondo (the Blonde one) and Enrico, had been denied access to a magisterial school (a teacher preparation school) (S. Gesualdi, 2007, p. vii), a fate that, as indicated in the preceding chapter, later befell three other students from the school. It had some influence on the *sessantotto* ('68) movement in Italy. It excited a number of activists and Italian intellectuals. As stated in the Introduction, these included the highly influential Pier Paolo Pasolini, who is captured on record expressing his enthusiasm for the book. The iconic Friulian poet, actor, writer, and film director called it a "wind of vitality," a book that provokes laughter following which tears come to one's eyes. He goes on to say: "I can say all the good things possible about this book. I have never felt so enthusiastic about something and then obliged, constrained to tell others: read it! The specific subject matter of *Lettera a una Professoressa* is the school but, in reality, it [the book] is about Italian society, present Italian life."[3]

Mario Capanna, formerly of Democrazia Proletaria and a leader in the '68 student movement during his student days at Milan's *La Cattolica* (Catholic University of the Sacro Cuore, Milan), wrote in 2007, the year that marked the *Lettera*'s 40th anniversary, of the huge impact that this book had on the student movements. It served as an important manifesto then in the struggle for reform of the Italian educational system. He feels that its impact confirmed how some of the more dynamic and social justice–oriented aspects of the Gospels had as much effect on the thinking then as some basic Marxist tenets in what constituted a strong combination of ideas in the struggle for reform (Capanna, 2007, p. civ)—shades of Freire, Latin America, and liberation theology!

Capanna feels that the *Lettera*, in an unadulterated form, should continue to have a telling effect today given the conservative reversal of policies in contemporary education (what we can generally regard as the neoliberal onslaught) and the intellectual stupor (we would see this as symptomatic of infotainment and "dumbing down") that characterizes the current scene (Capanna, 2007, p. cv). Another important educator in Italy, Domenico Starnone, author of the bestselling *Ex Cattedra* (1988) and *Appunti sulla maleducazione di un insegnante volenteroso* (1995),[4] whose writings even inspired such films as Daniele Lucchetti's *La Scuola* (The School), went so far as to declare, in the title of a piece he wrote for the ultra-left broadsheet *Il Manifesto* in 1992, that the '68 movement "broke out" at Barbiana (Starnone, 2007).

Many would argue that Milani also influenced the strong *Cattolici di sinistra* (Catholics on the left)[5] movement that continues to make its presence felt throughout the peninsula. Milani's influence was great among those who opted for a conscientious objection (*obiezione di coscienza*) with respect to military conscription. This stance has had a long-term effect on the lives of Italian youth. While the mandatory military conscription for males has been abolished in Italy, both male and female youth are still being allowed the option of engaging in community work (the alternative option to military conscription on the grounds of conscientious objection), financed by the Italian State, in any part of the world. In August 2011, one of us was a guest resource person at a session with popular educators involved in a project concerning the education of children in a shanty town at the periphery of Rio de Janeiro. A number of these popular educators were Italian young people benefitting from this opportunity provided by the Italian State.

Works have appeared, in both Italian and English, comparing Milani's ideas to those of Paulo Freire (see Mayo, 2007, 2011). The similarities between the two educators are uncanny despite the difference in contexts and time when both were active. One plausible explanation is that there had already been, by the time of Milani's involvement in education, a strong tradition of progressive education. As indicated in the preceding chapter, it was partly influenced by John Dewey's ideas of education for greater democratic living and new concepts deriving from various parts of the world, all indicating the dominative nature of much of what passes for traditional education. Just to give two examples, the anarchist Francesc Ferrer i Guàrdia (1859–1909) had long before left his imprint on educational thinking in Barcelona and the rest of Catalonia with his notion of the *Escuela Moderna* and had followers in the United States setting up modern schools. We have also seen how the pedagogical approaches of Célestin Freinet (1896–1966) were also well known. His use of the printing press and publication of newspapers suggest interesting possibilities for comparisons with Milani's approach involving the use of the daily newspapers and Milani's direction of sessions in which the students read newspaper articles and wrote back collectively. Freinet inspired the cooperative education movement to which Mario Lodi, who, in turn, introduced Milani to the idea of collective writing, made a contribution (Sessi, 2008, p. 153).

This is, however, all conjecture. What seems more plausible is that both Milani and exponents of critical pedagogy drew directly, in the former case, and indirectly, in the latter case, from the critique of bourgeois institutions that emerged from France. It is well known that Milani was *au courant* with French literature and specifically this type of literature from which critical educators were to draw via the writings of French sociologists and anthropologists. And there is a whole tradition in European socialist literature that exposes the bourgeois bias of public schooling and offers pedagogical and adult educational alternatives. We are sure ideas from this literature and the practice it records percolated through to educators such as Milani, Freire, Dolci, and others. In addition to all this, we must not lose sight of the fact that some of the more perceptive thinkers and practitioners in education and philosophy in general, committed to what Cornel West (Wells and West 2010) calls the pursuit of "unarmed truth," and "unconditional love," exhibit recurring traits the origins of which can be traced as far back as the ideas or reported ideas of ancient sages such as Socrates. One recent publication explores commonalities between Socrates' ideas in the *Apologia* (as reproduced by Plato), with its lifelong commitment to examining life in all its facets and denunciation of hypocrisy, and Milani and his students' collective rebuttal of accusations by the military chaplains and response to the judges regarding the Barbiana school's support of conscientious objection to military conscription (Centro Formazione e Ricerca Don Lorenzo Milani e Scuola di Barbiana, 2008). There is a common fount of inspiration among pedagogues and educationists in such classical works. They tend to transcend the historical epochs and geographical contexts in which they were written or spoken.

Underlying Common Influence: Radical Christianity

Like Freire, but unlike many other critical pedagogues of Anglo-North American stock, Milani's pedagogy is obviously Christian inspired, just as Socrates' ideas were inspired by belief in the revelations of God or conscience and a commitment to rejecting the temporal and superfluous material gains of life (Centro Formazione e Ricerca Don Lorenzo Milani e Scuola di Barbiana, 2008, p. 36). God's voice (in its Christian interpretation), revealed through conscience, is what drove Milani forward (see Corzo, 2011), even though he believed, despite his tribulations, in obedience to the Catholic Church and his Archbishop (M. Gesualdi, 2011b). That his pedagogy was Christian inspired goes without saying, given that Lorenzo elected to embrace the Catholic faith and take up Holy Orders. This was contrary to his parents' wishes. His mother who outlived him remained an atheist and had responded to the comment, by Lorenzo's wet-nurse, Carola Galastri, that it was great that both their sons became priests, with the brusque exclamation "bad milk" (Fallaci, 1993, p. 27). Once she had resigned herself to the fact that Lorenzo was bent on taking Holy Orders, she hoped that Milani would become a career priest rather than be content with serving as a village priest (*prete di campagna*) or, more appropriately, given his life's trajectory, mountain priest (*prete di montagna*) (Lancisi, 2007, p. 37).

Christianity, however, constitutes only one main strand in Freire's thinking. We come across a whole variety of influences in the Brazilian's work including one important influence, that of Marxism, comprising the work of Marx himself. One can safely say that two strands characterize Freire's work, namely Christianity and Marxism, which is typical of the radical Catholicism spread throughout and beyond his native Latin America, and which finds its ultimate expression in Liberation Theology. The same applies to other popular educators and intellectuals from that region and Freire's Brazil. It certainly applies to Carlos Alberto Libanio Cristo, better known as Frei Betto. The lay Dominican friar, on his own admission a disciple of Freire, is known for his writings and action for social and political reform in Brazil and for his direction of pastoral centers for leadership training in São Antonio, São Bernardo do Campo, and São Caetano, the metropolitan area of São Paulo (Betto, in Borg and Mayo, 2007, p. 35).

Milani is likewise eclectic in his writing and draws from various sources, but the underlying source in his work is that of Christianity with the main impetus deriving from the Gospels. We believe our preceding chapter makes this abundantly clear. While Marxist writers must have appealed to Milani and he used Gramsci's *Prison Notebooks* as one of the reading texts at the School of Barbiana,[6] there is no evidence of Marxist thinking serving as an important underlying current in his writings. The *Lettera*, written under his direction, is devoid of the sort of theoretical references one finds in, for instance, Freire's celebrated *Pedagogy of the Oppressed*, or the much "Marxified" later versions of Peter McLaren's popular introductory critical pedagogy text, *Life in Schools* (McLaren, 2006), not to mention many other texts written from the mid-1990s onward by this UCLA-based Canadian-born exponent of the field. The *Lettera* is arguably and deliberately less erudite than *Pedagogy of the Oppressed* in this regard. In our estimation, however, it is no less powerful in the force of its argument, arguably packing a stronger punch.

Milani's attitude toward socialism strikes us as being somewhat ambivalent. He criticized the Communist Party (PCI) and the Catholic Church for vying with each other and, consequently, selling young working-class people short in the various Italian localities with which he was familiar. In his view, they placed more emphasis on entertainment, such as carnival balls (Milani, 2004), than on education, with a view to swelling membership in the PCI's case or winning over souls in the case of the Catholic Church. The situation seemed to have reached ludicrous proportions typical of parish-pump politics in post–World War II Italy. This is the type of politics brilliantly satirized by Giovanni Guareschi (1908–1968) in his Don Camillo-Peppone series focusing on and around Brescello.

Milani had no problems with socialism as an ideology, despite his occasional reference to the excesses of the so-called *socialismo reale* (actually existing socialism) in the Soviet Union and the rest of the Eastern Bloc. In fact, Milani is on record as saying that democracy and socialism are "the two noblest political systems mankind has yet been given" (Milani, 1988a, p. 25). He considered socialism "the highest attempt of humankind to give, already on this earth, justice and equality to the poor" (p. 26).[7]

While Freire and other critical pedagogues (e.g., Stanley Aronowitz in New York City) were involved, at some periods in their life, in party politics (Freire, for instance, became a founding member of the socialist-oriented Workers' Party [PT] in Brazil and even served as Education Secretary in São Paulo on behalf of the PT while Stanley Aronowitz ran for governor of New York City), Milani had no such involvement. Milani and his pupils, writing in the *Lettera*, express an almost cynical attitude toward parties in Italy. They do not differentiate between the dominant parties in Italian political life, the "partiti dei laureati" (graduates' political parties) that allow representatives of the dominant social classes to legislate on behalf of the poor. "But we have to get into Parliament. The whites will never pass the laws that the blacks need" (Borg, Cardona, and Caruana, 2009, p. 107).[8] The assumption here is that even those parties that ostensibly represent the interests of the working class, the socialist and communist parties, are the preserve of the dominant classes. The thinking on this subject is conditioned by the particular situation obtaining in the Italian context, a situation in which members of the same family (e.g., the influential Berlinguer-Segni-Cossiga family from Sassari) can occupy leadership positions on different sides of the national political spectrum. This situation resonates with other countries and especially island states, as one of us would attest from his experience of living on another Mediterranean island state.

The authors also mention the mechanism whereby working-class and peasant-class people, who make it through the formal education system (and, for him, this included the seminaries), against the odds, and enter parliament, are often "embourgeoised" (*imborghesiti*) in the process. In the words of Edoardo Martinelli, Milani dreamt not of the "liberation" of people from farming but of a liberated farmer content with living a sober life (Martinelli in Borg and Mayo, 2007, p. 113), although, we ought to remark, this might not necessarily have been the intention of the boys' parents. The focus here is on raising the collective political and cultural level of a class rather than on individual "upward social mobility." The latter might well serve, in the end, to replace the personnel in the "contradiction of opposites," in Marx's sense of the dialectical relationship between oppressors and oppressed, but not terminate the exploitative relationship itself. As Gadotti, Freire, and Guimarães (1995) would say, power itself needs to be reinvented. Referring to a 1950 letter by Milani to the young Communist from Prato, Pipetta, Giuseppe Guzzo (1998) underlines that Milani shared with communists the struggle to combat the subjugation and abuse of the oppressed and redress the various injustices they suffer but would have parted company the moment these goals were reached (p. 123). We have shown earlier how members of the Florentine clergy did not read Milani's actions this way and there were those who considered him a "red priest." This precipitated his ultimate exile to the forlorn and "off the beaten track" Barbiana (Lancisi, 2007, p. 78).

These context-conditioned differences notwithstanding, there is something that strongly connects Milani's ideas concerning society and education to those espoused by exponents of critical pedagogy and critical education in general, namely, an underlying option for the oppressed and a commitment to an education for social justice (Borg and Cardona, 2008).

Gender and Other Forms of Difference

It would appear that the kind of critical education promoted at Barbiana was predominantly male oriented and rather gender exclusive, even though women, Olga and Carla, for instance, were also involved in the development of the text (S. Gesualdi, 2007, p. x). The generic names used to describe the haves and have-nots are male (Pierino and Gianni). This for some time was also a critique of critical pedagogy and especially Freire's early work, notably *Pedagogy of the Oppressed*. Even sympathetic writers such as bell hooks (1994) noted the "phallocentric" paradigm of liberation in Freire's most celebrated works, *Pedagogy of the Oppressed* and *Education for Critical Consciousness*. Such a criticism would probably be levelled at Lorenzo Milani also in view of the fact that, as we indicated earlier, the imagined target of his attack is a woman teacher (see Galea, 2010). Recall that the original intention was to write this as a protest letter addressed to the same teacher, a woman, who had thwarted the two Barbiana students in their attempt to join the magisterial school. This probably explains why they eventually opted for a more generic *professoressa* (woman teacher).

At the risk of sounding apologetic, we feel that the criticism regarding gender exclusiveness can be a trifle unfair. Lorenzo also spoke, albeit in a strong moralizing tone, about the dignity of women within what he denounced as a society gripped by the consumer culture ideology. One must also recognize his efforts to persuade parents from the region to send their daughters to the school at Barbiana. These efforts were frustrated as a result of the mentality that prevailed in the contexts where Milani worked, including the earlier context of San Donato. There was also fear of the dangers lurking in the areas around the road leading to the village of Barbiana, the sort of dangers that, the authors of the *Lettera* insisted, would have scared off those same teachers, from the public schooling system, who had flunked them.

> Not even one girl came from the town. Maybe it was because the road was hard. Maybe it's the mentality of the parents. They think a woman can live her life even if she has a chicken's brain. Males do not ask them to be intelligent. (Borg, Cardona, and Caruana, 2009, p. 39)

Later in the *Lettera*, however, we come across a passage setting high standards of attainment for what was conceived of as a "School of Social Service." The suggestion here is that gender exclusivity at Barbiana might have resulted from the school ethos. It was conceded that "Then as we go along, one could aim a little lower. Find a girl, adapt himself to love a more restricted family" (Borg, Cardona, and Caruana, 2009, p. 126).[9]

And yet we come across illustrations indicating that girls did attend this school (Milani, 2004, pp. 74–76), albeit a minority. They appear in illustrations such as that capturing an open-air geography lesson. This lesson involves help with reading provided by some of the youths of San Donato, thus indicating that links between the two schools, those of Barbiana and Calenzano, remained strong.[10] We are also shown a rather sex-stereotypical lesson on "cutting and sewing" (an "all girls" class). *Prima facie* it seemed as though the traditional gender stereotypes applied to this school.

The attempt, however, was to develop a school enriched by different identities. Italian society was at the time hardly the multiethnic society it is today. And yet this writing and other episodes from Milani's life seem to suggest a strong openness to matters concerning social difference. It is clear that Lorenzo Milani's sense of human solidarity extended beyond national, class, and gender boundaries. The notion of *patria* (Homeland) is given short shrift in his and the students' writings. It is also the object of repudiation with respect to its invocation, throughout history, which provided the licence for predatory incursions on defenseless foreign territories. This sense of repudiation is captured strongly in the letters to the judges and military chaplains. Students were sent to different territories abroad where they would mix with people of different cultures, something unlikely to have happened in and around Barbiana or the Italy of that time.

Metaphors chosen to describe the discriminatory nature of the power structure in Italian society, reflected in and exacerbated through the public schooling system, constantly refer to what were perceived as analogous situations in different parts of the world. They refer, for instance, to undemocratic race relations in the United States. Recall the earlier quote regarding embourgeoised parliamentary deputies and legislation. The Civil Rights Movement and the struggle for racial equality in the United States must have captured the imagination of the students at Barbiana. The reference to African American struggles, with prominence accorded to Stokely Carmichael, a key figure in the Civil Rights and Black Power Movements, also indicates that, in the authors' view, the range of solidarity among oppressed groups included solidarity with subaltern groups, and not only with those who suffer from class subjugation. One can here also mention the episode narrated by Edoardo Martinelli, in an interview with Carmel Borg and one of us, concerning patronizing European "missionary" treatments and representations of Africans:

> I recall that when a very good friend, Clara Urquhart, came to Barbiana for the first time and told us of her experiences in Lambaréne with Dr. Schweitzer, there was a heated exchange: "The Africans are not inferior beings" he [Milani] shouted "we only need to give them the instruments by which they can express themselves." These were times in which the west, through its strategies, annihilated, one by one and even physically, the various exponents of the anti-colonial liberation movements, thus preventing the birth of real nations with strong identities. (Martinelli, in Borg and Mayo, 2007, p. 114)

Furthermore, Milani's solidarity with oppressed groups knew no bounds. Despite his Jewish background, Milani was in no doubt regarding who were the impoverished in the struggle in and around Palestine that came to a head with the Six-Day War during his dying days in 1967. Again Martinelli captures his broad sense of solidarity with the "wretched of the earth," the "oppressed," when recounting this episode around what was shortly to become his deathbed:

> While he adopted a very aggressive attitude towards the rich, he was full of tenderness for those who suffered abuse of power. His sarcasm and sense of irony were unique. I vividly recall an episode that occurred in the room where he was to die two weeks later. We were all justifying Israel's involvement in the 6-Day War. And yet, with one eye opened and the other closed, he uttered in a faint voice: "It's the others who are the poor ones." This was followed by an immediate silence—a reflection that defied the logic of the arguments produced thus far. He was not concerned with who was militarily justified but continued to foreground the problem of social inequalities, the real reason behind every conflict! (in Borg and Mayo, 2007, p. 113)

As Filippo Toriello (2008, 2012) forcefully argues, the Barbiana experience offers strong insights for the development of a democratically inclusive and antiracist education that can contribute toward fostering inter-ethnic and multicultural (viewed in its broader contexts and not just confined to questions of ethnicity) solidarity.

Blood, Sweat, and Tears

One is likely to wince, when reading the *Lettera*, at the reference to the use of corporal punishment in extreme cases (Scuola di Barbiana, 1996, p. 82).[11] This has led to different interpretations. Our reading, however, is that, unlike the stroke of a pen that can ruin a person for life, this treatment would have no devastating effect on the child's future. This was also a time when corporal punishment was still used in many places in Europe in observance of the maxim: spare the rod, spoil the child. One form of punishment will be forgotten the next day while the other will be felt for an entire year (p. 83). Physical violence of this sort would be preferable to symbolic and structural violence.

One also notes the regime of austerity and discipline imposed by Milani at his school—perhaps a reflection of his Jewish culture? There is an austerity about Milani's approach to critical citizenship that would certainly not go down well with those accustomed to modern-day theories regarding the role of play in the process of human learning and development. It provides a contrast with the pedagogy of other priest educators such as Don Bosco, for instance, or of those educators who believed that "play is nature's way of learning." Part of the austerity is born of the fact that the area of "recreation" was slowly becoming a target of the growing commodification of the times, characterized by the consumerism emerging from the postwar Italian economic miracle (Pucci, 2007, p. 4). He feared that the widespread abandon to consumerist pursuits and delectation would lead human beings to their ruin since it would have a spiralling effect. This issue also greatly preoccupied Pasolini. As Edoardo Martinelli (2007) puts it, Milani educated his students to eschew excess and superfluity.

In this he was certainly prescient, given the pervasive contemporary effect of the consumer-culture ideology that dominates even such fields as education. Martinelli (2007) states that, on his deathbed, while looking at some of the children's photos, Lorenzo felt remorse for the austere pedagogical regime he imposed on them, the students to whom he dedicated his life. He broke down in tears and even asked for their forgiveness, feeling that he had exaggerated and was therefore mistaken; then came the warning, an immediate corrective, that the students will discover, on their own, that consumerism and fashion will create never-ending needs and that they will destroy, in human beings, any ideal or religious sentiment (p. 85).

As with a compatriot of Milani, Antonio Gramsci, this austerity is also based on another consideration, that working-class students need to work hard, shedding "blood, sweat and tears," to acquire that which comes almost naturally to middle-class children, more likely through what today are called "invisible pedagogies" connected with one's cultural capital and habitus. These privileged children are also referred to as the *figli di papà* (daddy's children) (see Borg, Cardona, and Caruana, 2009, p. 92) who make such institutions as the universities and parliament, each sustained through public funds, gained from the direct and indirect taxation of workers and peasants, appear as though they are their natural preserve.

There is a body of high status and powerful knowledge, as curriculum specialist Michael Young would put it, echoing Gramsci in many ways, that needs to be mastered. This mastery requires hard work involving, as Gramsci (1975) would write in the *Quaderni del Carcere* (Notebooks 4 and 12), specific psycho-physical habits. In denying working-class children access to this knowledge, one would be doing them the ultimate disservice. Milani, like Gramsci before him and Michael Young and Johan Muller after him (see Young and Muller, 2010), grasped this.

This explains his emphasis on rigor (not unlike Gramsci's proposals for a Unitarian school) and on long periods of study during and after conventional school hours and on weekends. It also explains his emphasis on alternative ways of educating pupils that makes them experience a sense of ownership of the learning program and see learning as fun and as being better than working long hours in the labor-intensive fields. Recall that Milani was to write with regard to the school schedule that city people are amazed at the schedule involved. Schooling occurred for 12 hours a day, 365 days a year. Recall also the rider he adds to this, namely, that before he arrived at Barbiana, the children observed the same schedule when working, enduring lots of fatigue in the process, with a view to providing city people with wool and cheese, underlining that therefore there was little to be cheerful about (Milani, 1988b, p. 54).[12]

As the students who wrote the *Lettera* disclose, "There was no break. Not even Sunday was a holiday" (Borg, Cardona, and Caruana, 2009, p. 36). There was little space for leisure pursuits. Milani encouraged skiing and swimming (thanks to the small pool constructed at Barbiana) but did so primarily, though not only, for their functional element—skiing connected farms to the school and swimming helped students overcome fear of water (Borg and Mayo, 2006, p. 140).

The austerity of the school, which reflected the austerity of Milani's life as a cleric, and his seminary preparation in Florence (life was reduced to bare essentials), was meant to underline the necessity for the laboring classes in Italy, as elsewhere, to "run while others walk," to adopt a famous slogan used in Tanzania during Julius Nyerere's presidency in the East African country.

Education, Politics, "Class Suicide," and Social Justice

Critical pedagogues have helped educators develop sensitivity to the politics of knowledge and to confront a disturbing question: On whose side am I when I teach/act? Freire (1985) tells us: "Educators must ask themselves for whom and on whose behalf they are working" (p. 80). Critical pedagogues, echoing the Brazilian, insist that education is not neutral and involves educating for either domestication or liberation. It involves taking sides. Being neutral means that one is siding with the dominant. While we readily associate this dictum with Freire and his followers, we need to bear in mind that there is a whole tradition, albeit repressed in certain quarters, of emphasizing this aspect of education that harkens back at least to the class struggles in education represented by that branch of proletarian education known in the English-speaking world as Independent Working Class Education. This also made its mark in Italy, certainly during the *biennio rosso* in Piedmont in the first quarter of the previous century and in nearby Germany, during Weimar Republic, not to mention England and Scotland with the emergence of the Plebs League concerning working-class education (see Waugh, 2009). This could not have been lost on Milani, another instance of the manner in which Milani and exponents of critical pedagogy drew from similar sources. Recall that, in his *Letter to the Military Chaplains*, Milani states forcefully:

> If you persist in claiming the right to divide the world into Italians and foreigners, then I must say to you that, in your view of things, I have no Fatherland. I would then want the right to divide the world into disinherited and oppressed on one side, and privileged and oppressors on the other. One group is my Fatherland; to me the others are foreigners. (Milani, 1988a, p. 19)[13]

In Martinelli's (2007) words: "There was obviously nothing really neutral about Don Milani. He believed in a committed educator, one who takes sides: 'Better a fascist than indifferent!'"(p. 113). This statement echoes Antonio Gramsci's famous and now popular declaration "I hate those who are indifferent" (*Odio gli indifferenti*), a statement so popular that it is emblazoned on Gramsci T-shirts sold at Ghilarza, in his native Sardegna, and other places. Echoing Amilcar Cabral, Paulo Freire and other critical pedagogues argue that revolutionary activists, and therefore revolutionary educators, need to commit "class suicide," that is, they must unlearn and renounce their privilege to work on the side of the oppressed, being *with* and not *for* them.

We wonder whether this is really possible and, if so, to what extent. It is not easy to underwrite the difficulties involved in "jumping out of one's skin." Perhaps the best one can hope for is to engage critically and persistently with one's contradictory consciousness. Don Lorenzo Milani came close to the idea of a person committing class suicide. He gave up his class privileges to dedicate himself to the poor and downtrodden in places he himself did not choose, including an isolated mountain community. His choice of living a life of poverty was deliberate, and he was careful that his lifestyle would not exceed the limits of that which characterized the life of his poor parishioners. Some commented about his apparent exaggeration in this regard, as if he wanted to overcompensate for his privileged upbringing (Lancisi, 2007, p. 58).

He denounced his education, which reflected his country's imperialistic ambitions. Here we refer to the famous quote cited at the outset of the previous chapter where Lorenzo denounces his own jingoistic education, which presented the empire as a "glory": *saltavo di gioia per l'impero* (I jumped with joy for the Empire). He denounced the element of deceit as information was withheld from the pupils' young impressionable minds by the teachers or curriculum developers at the time (Milani claimed to have been 13 years old then). They (the pupils) were not informed that poisonous gas was used against a defenseless people in Ethiopia who, with hindsight, appeared to Milani to claim the moral high ground since they had done nothing to the Italians while the latter, or rather their ruling war-mongering class, having already deceived the Southern peasant classes before (following the Risorgimento) by not distributing land, sought to expand their "empire" by inducing these impoverished peasants to take up arms with the hope of acquiring land in conquered African territories. In short, he denounced the school for its imperialist propaganda, predicated on lies and misinformation, and which prepared them as pupils and young citizens for the horrors that were to transpire during the Nazi-Fascist period during which no less than 50 million people, according to his estimation, died (Milani, 1988b, p. 65).[14]

Vilifying this type of schooling was no difficult task in the post–World War II years, given the then-widespread denunciation of the Fascist period. Milani, however, went a step further and held the social class to which he belonged responsible for the horrors of the imperialist wars (Milani, 1991, p. 42; Milani, 1988b, p. 62; Scuola di Barbiana, 1996, p. 74). *La borghesia ha scelto Mussolini* (the bourgeoisie has chosen Mussolini) is a common statement regarding the Fascist rise to power in Italy.

Despite being a Jew, an aspect of his set of identities rendering him and the rest of his family liable to persecution by the Fascists at the behest of Hitler, he was also a member of that same bourgeoisie that was responsible for the terrible turn of events in Italian politics. The commonly held view is that this class acted in such a manner to safeguard its privileges in a period characterized by a "crisis of legitimation." Milani therefore regarded the schooling of his childhood and adolescence as having been embroiled, as any public institution would have been, in the intrigue and class-ridden politics of the time. This no doubt was to have, in his mind and that of others, lasting residues that needed to be confronted head on. This emerges quite clearly in his and his students' reading of history "against the grain." This reading is strongly manifest in the letters to the military chaplains and the judges, both of which have pedagogical implications for the way we read and teach European history. It is the sort of reading/teaching/learning history against the grain that thinkers such as Gramsci, with his notes on Italian history and its politics of internal colonisation, as described in the *Quaderni del Carcere*, and more recently writers such as Pino Aprile (2010, 2011), have brought to the fore. This reading is intended to dispel myths and undermine the degree of sanitization and whitewashing, for instance, concerning the Risorgimento, which has extended beyond Italian shores to make it into the syllabuses for examinations elsewhere in Europe and the rest of the world. In short, there is a lot of pedagogical mileage in these letters to the judges and the military chaplains. Their focus is on the search for a "just war that does not exist" and therefore on reading history against the grain, as we find in the *Lettera*, *L'obbedienza non è piu una virtù* (Obedience Is No Longer a Virtue) and *Esperienze Pastorali* (Pastoral Experiences), the last two, unlike the *Lettera*, bearing Milani's sole authorship. This reading of history is intertwined with his reading of the history of the social class to which he belonged. The writings express his revulsion at the lengths to which this class would go to defend its privileges. This must have been the source of much fragmentation in Milani and can partly explain his renunciation, as far as possible, of the privileges associated with this class. We say "as far as possible" as a sobering reminder that one does not jump out of one's skin easily. Attempts at class suicide, in Cabral's terms, are fraught with deep contradictions. It is legitimate to assume that Milani, as with any other person in his situation, must have been lacerated by them.

We have noted how, in his later years as a priest, when visibly conscious of the fact that resources were limited and, once again, wary of the emerging consumerism at the time, Milani chose a life of sobriety, austerity, and poverty, a practical renunciation of the life to which he was born and in which he was bred. Once again, Edoardo Martinelli (2007) states: "He lived his sober life not as a form of penance, abstinence or simply Christian living but as a way of embracing the values and pleasures that can be satisfied and learnt only through poverty" (p. 112). And yet the earlier reference to the *partiti dei laureati* (graduates' political parties) would once again suggest that Milani and the Barbiana students would be among the first to recognize the limits of class suicide. Milani made similar remarks about seminaries that drew young men from the subaltern classes but then schooled them in a manner that made them cross to the other side of the river (Lancisi, 2007, p. 50), the same metaphor used by Freire in some of his statements expressing similar concerns (see Nita Freire, in Borg and Mayo, 2007, p. 3; Mayo, 2001). Milani and the students who authored the *Lettera* seem to doubt whether people from wealthy families can, despite their allegiances and ethical commitment to the subaltern classes, completely break away from their habitus.

These contradictions notwithstanding, Milani, like most critical pedagogues, would have regarded educating as a political act. Like them, he must have seen traditional educational institutions as bourgeois institutions and conventional teaching, marked by what Freire would call "banking education," as an activity that serves to support the status quo in a society marked by "cultural invasion" and what Pierre Bourdieu would regard as the "cultural arbitrary" of the dominant sectors of society. Repetition and ultimately exclusion were the case with the compulsory schooling of students from subaltern social strata in Italy during Milani's time. This was the experience of Gianni from whose point of view the *Lettera* is written. It is written in a tone of *anger* that results from the recognition of the "symbolic violence" meted out by a public school system that serves to reproduce class hierarchies. And yet we would underline that one of the points made strongly in the *Lettera* is that anger on its own does not lead to transformation and requires careful guidance and collective channelling into what we, for want of a better expression, would call productive action, the kind of pedagogical action that the students at Barbiana carried out under Lorenzo's conscious direction (*direzione consapevole*, as Gramsci would call it). Conscious direction must be predicated on a deep understanding of the underlying systemic social differentiation of which public schooling forms part. Feeling is to be allied with knowing as a prerequisite for transformative action and reflection.

The school at Barbiana was therefore conceived of as a place where students did not fail (Scuola di Barbiana, 1996, p. 80), failure having been identified by the authors of the *Lettera* as the weapon used by the school authorities to separate the Giannis from the Pierinos. This was regarded by the authors as anathema and denounced as anti-constitutional (Scuola di Barbiana, 1996, p. 61) in that everyone was entitled, according to the Italian Constitution, to several years of education, years that were not to be spent repeating the same class over and over again. Repetition and ultimately exclusion (a process of pushing out, euphemistically termed "dropping out") were the results of the compulsory schooling of students from subaltern social strata.

What is ostensibly a "fair" public education system, intended to provide opportunities for all citizens, according to the terms of the Constitution, is in effect a subtle way of reproducing the class system on the basis of a contestable notion of meritocracy:

> *Repetition classes.* If he knew it all, poor man, he'd get hold of the rifle again. There are some teachers who hold repetition classes at a fee. Instead of removing the obstacles, they work to increase the differences. (Borg, Cardona, and Caruana, 2009, p. 82)[15]

This book was therefore written as a clarion call for parents to organize themselves in a process of participatory citizenship intended to democratize public institutions such as schools.

> *Disarmed.* The poorer parents do nothing. They do not even imagine that these things happen. On the contrary, they feel moved. In their time, in the rural areas, there was only the *terza* class. (Borg, Cardona, and Caruana, 2009, p. 55)[16]

These schools are funded by the product of their own labors through taxes that many of them cannot evade, including such unfair consumption taxes as those imposed on basic necessities such as salt. What renders their situation ludicrous is the fact that they are paying for the salaries of teachers[17] who, instead of educating their children, act as judges who flunk them and push them out of the system.

> *The Tax System.* The curious thing is that the stipend used to throw us out is paid by us, the excluded ones.[18]

> The poor are those who consume all their income. The rich are those who consume only a part of it. In Italy, for an inexplicable reason, what one consumes is taxed up to the very last *lira.* Income tax is just a joke. (Borg, Cardona, and Caruana, 2009, p. 86)[19]

The schooling system, as countless educational sociologists have underlined over the years, backed by endless research, favors the "cultural capital" of the middle class. In contrast to the figure of Gianni, in the *Lettera*, we find that of Pierino, the "son of the doctor's" (p. 51), who enters school with a significant head start, who finds the scholastic experience a natural extension of the culture of the home, who moves easily through the various grades "and who found himself in the *quinta* class at nine years of age" (p. 69). He has time for leisure activities, meetings of the *Azione Cattolica,* or the *Giovane Italia* or the *F.G. Comunista* as well as time for his puberty crisis, the year of melancholy, the year of rebellion (p. 90).

Unlike Gianni, whose father "went to work at a blacksmiths when he was 12 years old and did not even complete the *quarta* class" (p. 80), Pierino can afford to have less formal schooling since he can avail himself of the materially rewarding cultural capital derived from home and its surrounding milieu (p. 48). This is the reason why Milani helped develop a school *a tempo pieno* (full time) at Barbiana, including weekends. Like Bourdieu and Passeron (1990), the authors of the *Lettera* state:

> You say that Pierino, son of the doctor, writes correctly. Of course you say so, he speaks just like you do. He is part of the firm. (p. 42)[20]

We are also told that Pierino is already branded "but this time with the brand of the prized race" (p. 62). Neera Fallaci (1993, p. 488) indicates how Milani, when writing about Pierino, had in mind his nephew, Andrea Milani Comparetti, who obtained 10 out of 10 in a History of Art Exam without studying anything. Andrea claimed in a published interview that he obtained the information on the 1400 and 1500 periods from a friend the evening before the exam. Andrea's friend obtained 6 out of 10 in the exam. In the interview, which Milani read, Andrea states that if the exams were a serious matter then he would not have obtained full marks. It was all a matter of being confident when facing the examiner in what was an oral exam (the Italian educational system entails sitting oral exams). It is all a matter of "selling oneself," according to Milani's nephew. On the other hand, Sandra Gesualdi (2007) also notes autobiographical elements in the figure of Pierino. She sees traces of *Lorenzino del dottore*, in short, a young Lorenzo (son of the Dottore, i.e., Dott. A. Milani) there, the one who would be dropped off some stops away from school not to be embarrassed in front of his mates who would see him being driven by a family chauffeur or the one who was pulled up for eating white bread in an alley inhabited by poor people (p. xi). She cites the following from the *Lettera* to illustrate the point, stating that this is exactly what the young Lorenzo did:

> *Disappear.* Poor Pierino, I almost feel pity for you. You have paid dearly for your privileges. Deformed by specialization, by the books, by your contacts with all the equal people. Why don't you go away? Leave university, the responsibilities, the parties. Start teaching immediately. Only language and nothing else. (Borg, Cardona, and Caruana, 2009, p. 111)

The eight authors of the text demonstrated the school's social class bias through a national award-winning piece of empirical research, one in which one of the boys Giancarlo, nicknamed "Tranquillo," played a prominent part, even greatly impressing two academics from the University of Florence who travelled to Barbiana to help with the stats (S. Gesualdi, 2007, p. lx). The authors identified, through a survey, the professions of the fathers of those children who grow old in the elementary school. The survey showed that "By failing the older ones the teachers have also hit the poorest ones" (Borg, Cardona, and Caruana, 2009, p. 71). When Gianni reached age 14 and was still at the first intermediate, continuing his formal education became "almost absurd" (p. 71). Bored, "when he is scolded for every penny he spends" Gianni would leave the much-hated school without acquiring any level of literacy. In a memorable line, the authors compare the public school to a hospital that treats the healthy and rejects the sick (p. 43).

In doing so, they denounce the teachers for their conditions of work. They allege that teachers work fewer hours than they ought to and should, as a result, be denied the right to strike, although they do suggest other forms of resistance and actions, to support the teachers' claims, that do not harm children. Passive, non-violent resistance à la Gandhi is one of them. The authors argue that teachers spend the extra hours giving private tuition to the Pierinos who can pay for such a luxury, thus widening the gap between the Pierinos and the Giannis. The gap is exacerbated, in the latter's case, by the lack of a congenial and materially rewarding cultural capital in the home and the surrounding milieu:

> In the morning they are paid by us to teach all equally. In the afternoons, they take money from the richer ones in order to teach their young gentlemen differently. In June, at our expense, they preside at the tribunal and they judge the differences. (p. 82)

The old intermediate school sharpened class distinctions chiefly through its timetable and its terms—short hours of schooling and long holidays. The direct effect of these structures is a school "cut to measure for the rich. For people who can get their culture at home and are going to school just in order to collect diplomas" (p. 20).[21] Following Milani, the boys advocated the establishment, across Italy, of a provision of after-school education:

> After school is a more fair solution. The child repeats but does not miss the year, he does not spend money and you are beside him in guilt and in suffering. (p. 100)

It is for this reason that the School of Barbiana entailed long hours of study throughout the week, including weekends. The concern with bridging the cultural capital divide invites parallels with Gramsci's advocacy of a Unitarian boarding school, in *Quaderni* 4 and 12, in which the senior students are also encouraged to teach the younger ones.

The Worlds of "Having" and "Being"

The school at Barbiana was a community school based on a very important consideration, namely, that a liberating and democratic education belongs to not the world of "having" but the world of "being." The authors would concur with many critical pedagogues, especially those who elucidate Freire's ideas, that there is no method and there are no techniques involved in providing this alternative type of education. Freire himself had rejected the "fetish of method" (see Aronowitz, 1993; Macedo, 1994; Macedo, in Freire and Macedo, 1995; Allman, 1996). We have seen, in the previous chapter, how Milani, for his part, responded when asked the irritating question regarding what was the key to the success of his approach at the adult education classes in San Donato. In his controversial *Esperienze Pastorali*, he claims that they ask the wrong question and that they should be preoccupied not with what *one has to do to teach* but with *how one should be* to teach (Milani, 1996, p. 80).[22]

It was all a question of "being," for Lorenzo Milani, rather than of "how to do." "Being" (Essere) entailed having clear ideas about social and political issues (Milani, 1996), the mark of those who educate for a critical citizenship. Here he seems to be in agreement with Freire's famous statement that "experiments cannot be transplanted but must be reinvented." Milani was adamant that the Barbiana experience cannot be reproduced elsewhere. It was an experience related to place and context. It started at Barbiana and was to end at Barbiana. Freire had spoken about reinventing the political pedagogical approach he promoted and not attempting to apply it cargo-cult style. The same applied to Barbiana. As far as we can understand, both Milani and the students he taught had faith in schools to change for the better. Some of them took up school teaching and had been vying to obtain a place at a teachers' preparation school. As one of us keeps telling student teachers, who read the *Lettera*, at his home university, the situation in public schools is different from that enjoyed at Barbiana. Milani had a free hand in that he was dealing with pupils already cast out of the system and who saw the time spent there as an alternative to hard work in the dirt inside the fields (*La scuola sarà sempre meglio della merda*—school is always better than cow shit). This is not the situation in the conventional public school system where teachers are constrained by a curriculum, syllabuses, time restrictions, and other requirements and situations connected with what is increasingly becoming a corporate world governed by corporate time rather than public time. The latter is the kind of time needed for Milani's *pedagogia della lumaca* (pedagogy of the snail). One has to reinvent the Barbiana approach, glean insights from the Barbiana experience, as indicated in the writings by the students collectively (the *Lettera*) or individually (Martinelli, 2007; M. Gesualdi, 2007), and allow these insights to inform the kind of approach adopted within the "limit situations" (Freire, 1970/1993) of the pedagogical setting in question. Pedagogy is context conditioned and is not something to be developed through a "one shoe fits all" solution.

Furthermore, the School of Barbiana connected *education* with *life*. The *Lettera*'s authors argued for an education that had to be culturally relevant and not culturally alienating. Edoardo Martinelli (in Borg and Mayo, 2007, p. 110) states that the *scuola dell'obbligo* (the compulsory public school) bored the life out of working-class children in his time there. In his words:

> The schooling of that period—I would dare say that the same could well apply to contemporary schooling—was based on the strict transmission of ministerial programs. These programs were carried out "to the letter" with the teacher being allowed little autonomy. Everything was planned to the extent that we students (there were several of us around, with different backgrounds) could anticipate the events, the questions and the title of the subjects to be tackled. We hardly came across anything that was unexpected and there were no situations that led to the adoption of pedagogical strategies that automatically connected with our interests, motivations and environments. The agenda was the same year in year out. I recall that I struggled to cope at school and I hated almost every subject.
>
> I could not perceive, at the time, the connection between learning and life. When I arrived at Barbiana, everything was different. The point of reference for the group's learning was life itself and this entailed an active research process. The learning setting itself was dynamic. [23]

We are told, in the *Lettera*, that:

> Gianni did not know how to write the "to have" verb. But he knew many things about the world of adults. About work, about families, about town life. Some evenings he went with his father to the Communist Party premises or to the Local Council sittings. [24]

> You, with Romans and Greeks, had made him hate all History. We could stay on for four hours without budging when we had lessons about the War. (Borg, Cardona, and Caruana, 2009, p. 41) [25]

Gramsci would beg to differ on this score indicating that knowledge of all aspects of previous civilizations is necessary if the working and peasant classes are to add a new link to the chain, a point that echoes Lenin's position in response to the *Proletkult* in Russia. The School of Barbiana provides other examples of what the pupils consider to be an irrelevant curriculum in the public school sector, one that does not valorize the pupils' abilities:

> During the Gym exams the teacher threw a ball at us and said, "Play basketball." We didn't know how. The teacher looked at us with disdain: "Unfortunate children."
>
> Even he is like you. The ability to perform a conventional ritual seemed important to him. He told the headmaster that we did not have "physical education" and he wanted to make us do a re-sit in September.

> We were all capable of climbing an oak tree. Once we'd be up there we wouldn't hold on and we'd chop down a branch weighing a tonne with an axe. Then we'd drag it on the snow up to the doorstep of our home and put it at mother's feet. (p. 52) [26]

Foreign language teaching and acquisition constitute one example of the manner in which Milani insisted on relating learning to life. He sent his pupils abroad to work in various cities and earn enough for their upkeep while they resided there; he secured funds for the Barbiana boys to cover their travel expenses. They had to pay for the rest by working abroad.

This was intended for them not simply to cross borders and broaden their horizons but also to learn foreign languages as spoken by the native speakers themselves. This approach stood in marked contrast to the artificial way by which foreign languages were taught and examined in the Italian public school system. Working- and peasant-class students often failed tests, the contents of which had no bearing on the kind of life lived within and outside the student's own region. As the authors of the *Lettera* say, the French learnt by Pierino, which enabled him to pass the state exam, would not allow him to find the way to the toilet in France (p. 45).

The focus here is on one's existential reality being the basis of one's coming into consciousness. In the words of Marx and Engels, "Consciousness is, therefore, from the beginning a social product, and remains so as long as men [*sic*] exist at all" (Marx and Engels, 1970, p. 51). As with Freire, who draws heavily on Marx and Engels, especially early works such as *The German Ideology* and *The Holy Family*, the starting point is always that of human beings "in the 'here and now,'" that is, the human beings' current situation "from which they emerge, and in which they intervene" (Freire, 1970/1993, p. 85). In Freire's adult education work in Angicos and elsewhere, learners and educators researched the community, exploring its pressing issues and codifying them. Teachers who joined his "popular public" schools project in São Paulo derived the generative themes from the surrounding community itself. They constituted "the building blocks for the construction of a locally relevant curriculum" (O'Cadiz et al., 1997, p. 85). Likewise, Milani used events or developments within the community that captured the students' imagination as motivating factors for lessons in a variety of areas. They constituted the *motivo occasionale* (the occasional motive). Martinelli (2007), who wrote a book on Milani around the title of moving from the *motivo occasionale* (the occasional motive) to the *motivo profondo* (the profound motive), discloses that, when he entered the classroom at Barbiana, he saw Don Milani and the rest of the class analyze skeletons in what was an anatomy lesson.

> The immediate motive, the key point of departure for his pedagogical activity, was provided by the fact that the floor of the society, which stood adjacent to the church, caved

> in. Bones were discovered as a result. The more profound and long term motive, as he explained in the *Letter To the Judges*, with reference to his pedagogical practice, was to avail himself of this particular event to capture the pupils' interest and thus gradually lead them, once they had become so motivated, to tackle the core areas of the disciplines. A few bones were sufficient to enable one to learn how to use vocabulary and texts dealing with anatomy and physiology. These subjects were non-existent in the middle schools of the period. This is how we learnt to read, write and count. (Martinelli, in Borg and Mayo, 2007, p. 110)

The operative word here is "lead" for the "here and now" constituted only the starting point of the lesson and was meant to lead to the disciplines: *Dal motivo occasionale al motivo profondo*: from the occasional motive to the profound motive. The occasional motive is just the starting point, however, and not the be all and end all of the pedagogical encounter (see also Freire, 1994, p. 84). In remaining there and not moving beyond (through co-investigation of the object of inquiry), and therefore not engaging in *praxis* (obtaining a critical distance from one's world of action to reflect on it for transformative action), one would be engaging in *basismo* (a form of populism, venerating the vernacular), as they would say in Latin America and especially in certain popular education circles where some of the major tenets of critical pedagogy were born. They had to move from there not to any specialized curriculum that mortgages the child's future, the kind of curriculum introduced by Giovanni Gentile's ministry in the Fascist period that Gramsci had denounced in prison, but to a more general curriculum. The Barbiana boys were against early specialization, as this would limit Gianni's possibilities for further learning and growth.

> If he has a passion for a subject one should forbid him to study it. Tell him that he is limiting himself or that he will not be rounded out. There's lots of time later to close oneself in specialisation. (Borg, Cardona, and Caruana, 2009, p. 98)

The best way to engage the learner's framework of relevance is to allow space for the learners themselves to engage critically with the issues, to bring their own insights, culture, and different aspects of their multiple subjectivities to bear on the learning process. This is the antithesis of "banking education" and the ministerial programs to which Martinelli refers.

This process of learning serves as an antidote to the kind of boring and alienating education associated with the "banking" type of education, the kind of education that led the Giannis or Giannas to be pushed out of the public schools in Italy after they flunked their summative exam. Like Buber, Freire, and other critical educators, Milani believed in dialogical exchange and the *conferenza del venerdi* (the Friday conference) at San Donato provided an excellent example. Workers and peasants prepared the material beforehand to avoid being ostensibly passive listeners (as Gramsci, Freire, and others have shown, one is never really a passive listener since one derives different meanings from what is being presented without necessarily giving voice to this meaning). They were encouraged to engage the speaker. Milani often pulled up the speaker for a lack of adequate preparation and communication, as is evident from a letter to a certain Dott. Gozzini (Milani, 1970, p. 37).

Milani practically formalized the students-teachers roles at Barbiana for logistical as well as pedagogical reasons. He introduced peer tutoring/teaching, realizing that pupils often learn better from their own peers with whom they share the same social class, broader cultural background, and language. It has been argued that one enhances one's learning by communicating what is learnt to others. At the Barbiana school, those who did not keep pace were helped to learn by their peers who, in turn, enhanced their understanding of what was learnt through the effort involved in conveying it to others. "Communicating your ideas to others enables you to clarify and elaborate them" (Bonanno, 2002, p. 97). One learns and consolidates the learning of things best by teaching them to others.

In a school that placed the emphasis on caring, with the motto "I Care" written on one of the school walls in English (Milani, 1991, p. 34; Milani, 1988b, p. 56), the students engaged in a pedagogical experience in which they were both teachers and learners. Milani himself tutored the first group of students. As students increased in number—there were around 40 students in one particular summer—he adopted peer tutoring as a key pedagogical tool. This brings to mind, for one of the authors of this text, his experience as a student teacher teaching mathematics at a vocational school in his home country (Malta) in the late 1970s. The school, known as a "trade school," was a repository of students who attended ostensibly for vocational purposes but many of them were in reality pushed out of the mainstream school system. There was a difference in the rate of learning exhibited by the students when working out mathematical exercises. Some finished earlier than others. To avoid the mayhem and disruption that these students would have caused, the author would pair them with classmates who experienced difficulties in grasping concepts. He did so to help the latter with their tasks. In all honesty, the author would be the first to admit that the students did a better job than he did in communicating the tasks at hand not least because they were of the same social class and spoke the same regional language as the other students. Both sets of students connected with a similar framework of relevance. This is something that the author as teacher was denied through his class *habitus*, age, and "grammar of taste" (in Bourdieu and Passeron's sense). There is also the kind of language code that teachers need to observe but that pupils certainly ignore especially when whispering to each other. While there was a difference in purpose between Milani's attempt at peer tutoring and the one just described—one of the author's main concerns was classroom control—the effectiveness and meaningfulness of peer tutoring could not have been lost on him. This experience obtained greater resonance many years later when the author read the *Lettera* for the first time. It also echoed Maria Montessori's similar efforts at peer tutoring. This pedagogical approach, consisting of enabling students to teach each other, allows for the emergence of what Lev Vygotsky would call "zones of proximal development." Of course this approach can be traced as far back as at least the 'monitorial system' used by the 18th-century Quaker John Lancaster at his school in London.

At Barbiana, the older students, while learning from Milani and other students of more or less the same age, also taught the younger ones.

> There was only one copy of each book. The boys used to crowd around it. It was hard to notice that one was a bit older and was teaching. The oldest of those teachers was sixteen years old. The youngest was twelve and I was full of admiration for him. I decided from the first day that even I would teach. (Borg, Cardona, and Caruana, 2009, p. 36) [27]

Older students could spend a whole morning teaching their younger counterparts.

> The following year I was a teacher. That is, I was a teacher for three half-days a week. I taught Geography, Mathematics and French to the *prima media* class. (p. 37)

Here was a "caring" educational relationship based on learning not for one to have (possessive knowledge and individualism) but for one to be and to be for others. It must have served as a tremendous source of motivation for the students, once degraded and therefore demoralized by the public schools, to now be elevated to the status of and esteemed as teachers. It is hardly surprising that they would prefer these experiences to the messy ones encountered in the fields (p. 36; Scuola di Barbiana, 1996, p. 13). This source of motivation made them serve as educators as well as learners in the same way that cultural circle members, as presented by Freire, in a process that influenced critical pedagogy, served this dual role through a process of "authentic dialogue."

An authentic dialogical approach necessitates the sharpening of listening and observation skills. I would here point to the quote in the previous chapter from *Esperienze Pastorali* in which Lorenzo Milani states that he derived many insights and ideas from the peasants themselves. As indicated in the previous chapter, he claims that he owes everything that he knows to the young workers and peasants with whom he carried out schooling. He states that it is he who learned from them that which they believe to be learning from him. Recall that he goes on to assert that he only taught them to express themselves while they have taught him how to live and that it was they who led him to think those thoughts that are expressed in the book. Milani states that he wrote them because they [the workers and peasants] placed them in his heart (see Milani, 1996, p. 76).[28]

Milani also believed in a directive form of education, the alternative to which would have been laissez-faire pedagogy, denounced by many critical pedagogues including Paulo Freire, Ira Shor, and Henry Giroux. Allowing his students to indulge in laissez-faire pedagogy would have been a case of utter irresponsibility on Milani's part, given the age of the students at Barbiana and Milani's concern for their future in a society where knowledge is power. Having said this, he believed in the students' autonomy as learners. When he left San Donato and took up residence in Barbiana, the Friday conference continued to be carried out by the youths of San Donato themselves. He assisted them from afar by establishing contact with potential speakers, as indicated in one of his letters to Elena Brambilla, dated June 20, 1961 (Milani, 1970, pp. 147–148). We have seen, in the preceding chapter, that, two years later, the Curia prevented Don Milani from speaking at a conference at S. Donato di Calenzano (Sessi, 2008, p. 158). This occurred precisely nine years following his removal from there. Don Milani had been invited by the locality's mayor to speak at a conference concerning the possible setting up, in the locality, of a *doposcuola,* an after-school program for students in need of help with their school work (M. Gesualdi, 2011a, p. 17). Milani also had faith in the Barbiana boys' ability to learn on their own by working and living abroad, for a period of time, in places located not only in Europe but also in North Africa.

The emphasis on exchange of views and learning from each other in the learning settings that Milani helped create together with community members (at San Donato) and his students (at Barbiana) throws into sharp relief an important aspect of an education intended to serve as an antidote to that which predominates in a capitalist world. Milani, anticipating the critical pedagogy tradition, underlined the *collective* dimensions of knowledge. There are those who connect this approach with that of "cooperative learning" (Abbate, 2008), probably because the person who inspired it, the elementary school teacher Mario Lodi, belonged to the cooperative education group (Sessi, 2008, p. 153). This collective writing approach remains relevant in an age when we are bombarded with such phrases as "self-directed learning," "individualized modules," and a language that conceives of us as atomized individuals.

The School of Barbiana provided a learning space that affirmed the collective dimensions of learning in contrast to the dominant compulsory school that promoted a notion of citizenship predicated on the ideology of competitive individualism typical of capitalist social relations. The "I Care" motto points to this. The program at Barbiana was based on a politics of solidarity and caring. Not only did pupils care but we have seen how their caring also took the form of a collective pedagogical experience in which they were both teachers and learners. Furthermore, the chronicles of the time served as an important source of learning at Barbiana. The afternoon lesson at Barbiana was common to all. It centered on the facts of the day as reported by the local newspaper. Here the newspaper constituted an important teaching resource, as was the case with the Scuola Popolare of San Donato di Calenzano (Simeone, 1996, p. 105). This lesson combined knowledge of current affairs with the teaching of such skills as critical analysis and *critical literacy*, to borrow a term from Paulo Freire that constitutes a key aspect of critical pedagogy. This represents an attempt to read the world through a critical engagement with this world's *construction* via the media:

> I also knew well the historical period in which I lived. That is the newspaper that, at Barbiana, we read every day, aloud, from top to bottom. (Borg, Cardona, and Caruana, 2009, p. 49)

Milani and the students followed current events and controversies, engaged collectively with articles, identifying their underlying ideological positions, as Freire would put it, and this exercise in critical literacy often provoked *collective* responses by the students working in concert with their mentor. The same applied to other collective endeavors attesting to their sense of critical literacy. This includes the *Letter to the Judges* in which Milani constantly refers to discussions with his students concerning the many points made throughout the letter, including the several points based on a critical reading of history, one that went against the grain, in contrast to the history learned in the public schools (Scuola di Barbiana, 1996, p. 123).

Echoing a point made by Paul V. Taylor (1993) with respect to Freire's notion of "reading the word and the world," the Barbiana pupils not only *read* but also *wrote* the world and, we would add, they did so *collectively* and *critically*. All this was intended to transmit to students the self-confidence to be live wires on which nobody can tread—a reflection of Milani himself. This is a tall order for children who hail from a traditionally subaltern class that has traditionally shown deference to its social betters, including those who speak on its behalf. Milani, for his part, was always a status-quo disturber and hard to subdue (*scorbutico*). With his incisive critical inquisitiveness that landed him in hot water with civic and ecclesiastical authorities, not least in his seminary years, Milani displayed all the confidence, *savoir faire,* and *savoir dire* that derived from being born and raised in the *classe dirigente* (ruling class). Once again, the earlier discussion, focusing on Bourdieu and

Passeron's adopted notion of habitus, becomes relevant here. The collective critical dimension was intended to create the right milieu for the subaltern to learn to exercise their "right to govern," to become *cittadini sovrani* (sovereign citizens). [29]

Perhaps the major contribution to an education with a collective dimension is provided by the following feature of the teaching/learning process at Barbiana. In keeping with the "I Care" motto at the school, the class did not proceed to the next stage in the learning process until every pupil mastered the last one. Rather than fail pupils, the school gave priority to the child who fell back. As argued elsewhere (Borg and Mayo, 2006, p. 143), "unlike elitist educational systems which stream and track students according to perceived 'ability,' creating in the process the context for high expectations for largely privileged students (the Pierinos/as) and lower expectations (a 'cooling out' process) and less resources for mostly working class, disabled and nonwhite students," the Barbiana School gave priority to those who fell behind. The Barbiana School is instructive regarding "how educational institutions, especially those run by the Church, can consciously choose to educate the least privileged as part of a genuine option for the poor" (Borg and Mayo, 2006, p. 143):

> However, whoever lacked the basics, who was slow or unmotivated, felt that he was the favourite one. He was welcomed just as you'd welcome the first in class. It seemed as if the school existed solely for him. Until he understood, the others did not move ahead. (Borg, Cardona, and Caruana, 2009, p. 36) [30]

The Barbiana School favored an education system that, involving a collective group effort, does not give up easily on the child:

> You would wake up at night with your thoughts directed straight to him in order to find a new way of schooling, which is cut to measure for him. You'd go and look for him in his house if he did not come back. (p. 98). [31]

The authors warned against streaming (tracking in the United States) practices as suggested by a member of the Christian-Democratic party, who, in a speech in parliament, unabashedly argued: "Why on earth should those who are intellectually gifted and motivated be humiliated in a school where it is necessary to clip their wings, in order to keep them at the flight level of those who by nature must necessarily proceed slowly?" (Borg, Cardona, and Caruana, 2009, p. 88). Alas, many share this view in this day and age, all in keeping with a concept of citizenship characterized by "survival of the fittest" in a jungle of competitive individualism. Being true to the message of the Gospels, Milani and his students opted for a process of education in which, once again, one learns not to have but to be and be for others. Learning was to be shared with others.

This standpoint provided elements that add credibility and forcefulness to the arguments developed throughout the *Lettera*. Certainly teachers play an important role in providing a social justice education predicated on an option for the poor and less-privileged members of society. They are not the only important players in this process but nevertheless their role remains crucial. This explains why people who promote a critical approach to education accord a strong sense of agency to socially conscious educators acting as transformative cultural workers (Giroux, 1988a) "in and against" a bourgeois-oriented and therefore biased school system.

And while Freire provides edifying images of teachers, whose conditions he sought to improve when education secretary in São Paulo, one comes across a different image of teachers in the *Lettera*. These are persons who flunk students, assess them on skills they did not enable the students to acquire. The authors humorously point to the teacher's inane assertion that writers are born and not made, to which, in a classic example of skillful repartee, they retort: "But in the meantime you earn your salary as *a teacher of Italian*" (Borg, Cardona, and Caruana, 2009, p. 137; Scuola di Barbiana, 1996 (p. 125 [32]). In fact, the students indicate that writing is an art that needs to be learned, a point that recalls Bourdieu's stricture concerning the fact that pupils are often assessed on skills and qualities (style) that are not taught but that often reflect class distinction (1976). The *Lettera* provides insights into the systematic way through which students engage in collective writing, the technique that drew interest from different parts of the region and which motivated Adele Corradi, a public school teacher who helped Milani at his school on her free days, to make the trip to Barbiana in the first place. On her own admission, she found the teaching of writing tough going in her daily teaching at her public school (Corradi, 2012, pp. 13–16). The students at Barbiana were encouraged to place all their random ideas on sheets of paper; a systematic ordering and sifting then occurred, through collective discussion, until some key non-repetitive ideas remained to allow for a coherent piece of writing. They eliminated superfluous words, redundancies, and overly long sentences and made sure not to have more than one concept in a single sentence (Borg, Cardona, and Caruana, 2009, p. 139).

> At Barbiana I had learnt that the rules of writing are: to have something important to say and that it may be useful to everybody or to many. To know who you are writing to. To gather all that is necessary. To find a logical way of putting it in order. To eliminate any unnecessary word. To eliminate any word which we do not use while speaking. Not to set any limits of time. (Borg, Cardona and Caruana, 2009, p. 44)

Lessons from Lorenzo Milani and the San Donato/Barbiana Experiences

Did the School of Barbiana give up on teachers in the public school system? On the contrary, the School of Barbiana experience provides an alternative form of schooling from which teachers in the public school system can learn. Much depends on the attitude that the teachers develop, as indicated by Milani when he says it is more a question of how one must be, rather than what one must do, to be able to teach in a manner that is meaningful to one's students. Teachers can provide such an alternative education by

- calling for and engaging in a *doposcuola* (after-school) program that is provided to everyone and not just those who can pay for it;
- striving and clamoring for different ways of making the school accessible, including physical accessibility;[33]
- encouraging peer tutoring;
- enabling students to learn collectively and "to be" not just for themselves but also and mainly for others;
- relating education to life; by starting with the "here and now" and moving beyond to *higher order* thinking through what today would be termed "productive pedagogies";
- engaging *with* learners in a critical reading of the world (*praxis*) as manifest in its daily reality but also through its construction via the media;
- being disposed to learn and relearn what they think they already know from the pupils themselves who have a lot to offer in terms of insights derived from their different cultural backgrounds and specific abilities;
- calling for an inclusive curriculum that is relevant to the different pupils in the classroom;
- calling for a school that does not fail students and push them out but ensures that the constitutional right of everyone to enjoy a number of years of public schooling (that do not involve repetition) is respected and safeguarded.

The fact that some pupils from the Barbiana experience aspired to become and some did become teachers indicates that they had faith in the emergence of a type of teacher who was different from the one portrayed in a negative light in the

Lettera. They had faith in a teacher concerned with social justice issues and who sees her or his mission in life as one intended to improve the life chances and experiences of those who have traditionally suffered in a socially differentiated system. This is the type of teacher that the School of Barbiana sought to inspire. And the verb "calling for" in the first in the list of qualities just provided indicates that many of the challenges cannot be faced by teachers on their own. As many critical pedagogues would argue, they can only be faced by teachers within a movement or alliance of movements, involving people from other walks of life, including the parents called on in the *Lettera* to organize themselves and clamor for reforms in the state school system that would thus help revitalize an important sector of the public sphere.

4

Writing as Collective Literacy

"L'indicibile dei vinti / il dubbio dei vincitori"
(The unspeakable of those who have been defeated / the doubt of the winners)
—Pietro Ingrao

The Barbiana school contributes to the history of critical pedagogy a radical example concerning how to provide a space for "voice and empowerment" (Giroux, 1988b). While the Italian school is still mainly concerned with "learning to read," the Barbiana school provides effective socioeconomic narratives that reflect a proper ability in "reading to learn" (Smith, 2003).

In the same years that scholars such as Jerome Bruner were enhancing the fundamental role of narrative structures and of constructivist perspectives concerning the process of thinking, the writing of Lorenzo Milani and the writings of his pupils provided concrete and effective examples of how education can strengthen such a process through shared collective efforts. Such efforts always seem to respond with precision to what William Labov (1972) terms the two fundamental components of narrative structure: What happened? Why is it worth telling?

In a letter (quoted by F. Gesualdi and Corzo Toral, 1992, pp. 17–18) dated March 16, 1966, addressed to Ms. Dina Lovato, Lorenzo Milani focuses on the *Letter to the Judges* (October 18, 1965). He comments to her that

> We wrote the "Letter to the Judges" as if we were working to produce a masterpiece. Unfortunately very few people seem to notice it among the hundreds who wrote to us from

Italy and from abroad. They all think that we have the most beautiful ideas. Very few, maybe only two or three people seem to be aware that in order to clarify our ideas to ourselves and to the others we need to work all together for months just to produce a few pages. If everybody would do so, everybody would be able to write like we do, and there would be no need to revere us as if we were blessed by God's grace. Anybody can have the grace to measure his or her own words, cluster them, delete repetitions and contradictions, as well as useless things, in order to choose the words that result most true, most logical, most effective.

As this chapter will address, Milani's concern for the role of his pupils as knowledge co-producers and the idea that such production should result in a masterpiece is of fundamental importance for his educational work. In Milani's view the achievement of a masterpiece level is related to the ability to ask and to answer relevant questions by children whose culture—the culture of peasants and workers—is usually neglected and nonetheless bears a vital transformative potential. In the first place such a transformation process should challenge the bourgeois oppressive power and dominant cultural patterns legitimizing this power structure. Milani's letter (as quoted in F. Gesualdi and Corzo Toral, 1992, pp. 17–18) goes on to say:

> It is necessary to reject any concern in relation to politeness, interest, bourgeois upbringing, convenience. It is necessary to ask for the advice of many people concerning how to be effective. Eventually in this way what is being written becomes clear for both those writing it and those reading it. The *Letter to the Judges* has been a gift that we have received and that we have offered. Before writing it neither me nor the pupils knew those things. We were feeling them.... The effort to express the truth that is just being felt makes it possible to reveal such a truth to ourselves and to the others.

Although Milani and Freire never met or corresponded with each other, the former's words seem reminiscent of the Brazilian's. The concepts of word, life, change are linked together as if to appear synonymous. Both were concerned with being with the oppressed rather than imposing on them any school model. They place dialogue at the core of their pedagogy, and they are sensitive to personal relations and at the same time to the need to give birth to a collective process.

In *"La parola fa uguali"* (The word makes us equal, M. Gesualdi, 2005) Milani is reported to have said that in his educational work he had to learn a language that he did not know and how to teach Italian grammar without indulging in any complex quote or elaboration. When he talks and he writes about his educational work, Milani seems concerned with finding ways to facilitate learning without falling into the usual teaching traps that turn communication into a representation of communication itself. He is concerned with finding an emancipatory language. This language can only be found by giving up the role of the one who knows and by triggering his pupils' narrative abilities. Milani offers us not a model but rather a way of being with the learners. When it comes to the art of writing, the Barbiana school provides examples that are at the core of critical literacy. As Williams (2012, p. 18) states:

> Critical perspectives encourage the deconstruction of test and meaning in society until it becomes a means for understanding one's own history and culture, to recognize connections between one's life and the social structure, to believe that change in one's life, and the lives of others and society are possible as well as desirable, and to act on this new knowledge in order to foster equal and just participation in all the decisions that affect and control our lives. This paves an important path for educators and others working for social change and will provide the necessary language and strategies that challenge many Positivists' theories which advocate a persistent disempowering of learners in our schools and the marginalization of large numbers of Americans. Critical literacy transcends conventional notions of reading and writing to incorporate critical thinking, questioning and transformation of self or one's world. Additionally, definitions of critical literacy usually consider "text" to be anything that can be "read," which leads to infinite possibilities.

The letters written at Barbiana clearly state that education is more than schooling, especially when schooling is based on the idea of the canon offered by a textbook and teacher while the pupils are mainly passive receivers of this imparted knowledge. According to Lorenzo Milani, to initiate empowering collective writing does not imply that the teacher becomes just one of the pupils. He maintained a sense of responsibility with regard to leadership. Nonetheless, he worked toward fostering distributed leadership. In relation to the content of the collective writing, since he was bent on providing a space for the pupils' culture to express itself and to evolve through mutual exchanges, he adopted a position of "ignorance." Such a position makes us think of *The Ignorant Schoolmaster*, written by Jacques Rancière, about a French revolutionary teacher of the 1820s and 1830s, Joseph Jacotot. According to Jacotot the best schoolmaster should be "ignorant." His or her role should be to set the stage for a process of learning that is beyond his or her control. Being ignorant of the subject matter helps the schoolmaster not to impose his or her understandings on the pupils' discussion, which should be based on the principle of freedom over which the revolutions of the late 18th century were fought. Self-transformation (Giroux and McLaren, 1994)—as described by Paulo Freire as well—is at the core of this educational approach and is therefore going to be a recurring issue throughout this chapter. As Lave and Wenger (1991) put it, "Hegemony over resources for learning and alienation from full participation are inherent in the shaping of the legitimacy and peripherality of participation in its historical realizations. It would be useful to understand better how these relations generate characteristically interstitial communities of practice and truncate possibilities for identities of mastery" (p. 42).

Individuals do not learn by themselves. This concept was expressed by Vygotsky and supported by his studies and later by scholars such as Lave. We learn with others, and we are strongly influenced by social worlds. These social worlds are built collectively, and they play a key role in determining what should be known and how. To Lorenzo Milani it is clear that learning is a political process, and learning implies some form of teaching. The form of such teaching plays a crucial role. From this perspective the work at the Barbiana school is also one that addresses theories of culture, as well as theories of hegemony.

In France, almost in parallel to the work evolving at the Barbiana school, Pierre Bourdieu was developing his social theory placing the school in a key position in the process of reproduction of class segmentation (1970/1977) and related "cultural" patterns. While for scholars such as Cremin it was important to analyze the diachronic transformation of the school and to place such changes within the school contexts, Bourdieu was concerned with the modern polity and therefore focused on the synchronic "arbitrariness" of schooling as a process that would move the young into adult positions. What seems important in Bourdieu's work in relation to collective writing as an act of resistance and cultural change is the French sociologist's attention to the violence that accompanies the imposition of any culture on a human group. Bourdieu's views seem particularly relevant to appreciate the Barbiana school's collective writing approach as he focused on and emphasized the relationships among controlled and controlling agents (teachers, parents, students) within the schooling process. From this sociological perspective pedagogies are the methodologies that these agents of the school use and that are performing specific forms of authority (to teach and to evaluate), on the basis of specific forms of legitimacy.

Writing as an Art Form

The first narrative about the collective writing method by Lorenzo Milani is a letter dated November 2, 1963, and addressed to teacher Mario Lodi. It was published by Lodi four years later in "Cooperazione Educativa" (July–August 1967, pp. 3–9), the review of the Italian Movimento Cooperazione Educativa (MCE). It is also included in Lodi's *Il paese sbagliato* (1970, pp. 458–466) and later in "Lettere" (pp. 147–197) and in Gesualdi and Corzo Toral's *Don Milani nella scrittura collettiva* (1992, pp. 26–33).[1] A primary school teacher in Vho, Lodi had been visiting Milani during the summer of 1963.

> I met Don Lorenzo in 1963 thanks to my friend Giorgio Pecorini.—Lodi recalls—His educational work is being spoken of today as a modest countryside school but in reality it was a top quality school. It was a part of Italy that was living its freedom in an autonomous

way. Don Milani was the first one to launch the idea of a universal school—the idea of transforming the school into a democratic tool—but not many have understood the depth of his thought. (interview with Mario Lodi, *la Repubblica*, February 16, 2012)

A primary school teacher from 1948 to 1978, Mario Lodi was concerned with showing how the Italian school could be democratized and transformed from within. Some of his books are dedicated to recording the work of his pupils throughout the school years. Their diaries and school works are presented in four volumes: *C'è speranza se questo accade al Vho* (If this is happening in Vho there is still hope), *Il paese sbagliato* (The wrong town), *Insieme* (together), and *Il mondo* (The world), a collection of the newspapers edited and published by his pupils over five years.

Although the formal author of the books is Mario Lodi, it is the pupils who are the actual writers of most of the texts included in these volumes. As in the case of Barbiana, the "culture" is actively constructed by the pupils. The *cultura del bambino* (child's culture) is the main topic of Lodi's pedagogical writings. Along with Gianni Rodari and the pedagogical innovative approaches developed by local authorities such as that of Reggio Emilia, Lodi had an open mind concerning the plurality of children's creative languages, and he viewed "mistakes" as learning opportunities. Even the title of *Il paese sbagliato* (The wrong town) suggests a creative use of "mistakes," and he encourages an awareness of the multidimensional and polysemic written and visual productions by his pupils who are encouraged to provide their own perceptions and understanding of their own reality through drawings and texts and to compare each other's representations. The representation of a town can be "wrong" because it lacks the appropriate scale, but most importantly a town is "wrong" when it does not tackle inequalities. Lodi's pupils were encouraged to actively explore their environment and to conduct and record interviews. Both Milani and Lodi were keen to expose their pupils to information and communication technologies and to apply them to their research work. It must be noted that the Barbiana school did not have electricity until September 1965, that is, 11 years after Lorenzo Milani's arrival. Once able to use electric power, Lorenzo Milani did three things. He bought a semi-industrial washing machine, finally relieving Eda from some of her heavy work. He asked a friend who worked for Olivetti to provide the school with electric typing machines and electric calculators. He borrowed a 16 mm movie projector. This allowed him to rent and to project some of the best movies to watch together with the pupils to analyze and deconstruct some of them.

Milani and Lodi agreed to encourage their pupils to exchange letters. The first one was written by the Barbiana pupils at the beginning of the 1963–1964 school year and it reached Lodi's pupils in November 1963.

It took the Barbiana pupils nine days to draft their first collective letter. In its accompanying letter, written on November 2, 1963, Lorenzo Milani highlights that the actual letter includes 823 words while halfway through the collective writing process it included 1,128 words. An English translation of part of Lorenzo Milani's accompanying letter is included in Borg, Cardona, and Caruana (2009, pp. 216–217):

> Dear master,
> I enclose the letter. I thank you for proposing this idea to us because I felt myself at ease using it. In all these years I have been teaching I have never had such a complete and deep reaching occasion to study the art of writing with my students. So everything is fine for us. I'm even very enthusiastic about it. On the other hand I'm afraid the letter will not suit you. Being all immersed in the study of the maximum level of ability of expression of these children, we forgot somehow about the age of the readers.

The Letters to Mario Lodi's Pupils

Lorenzo Milani then wrote a long preface describing how the letter was written (Milani, 2007, pp. 207–211) and explaining that the drafting of the letter took nine days:

> The first day
> We dedicated to it the whole afternoon, five hours. Individually, each of us wrote a letter to you answering the question "Why do I come to school?"
>
> The second day
> Again, we dedicated the whole afternoon to it. We went through all the letters by reading them aloud. As we were reading them, the most interesting sentences and ideas were copied onto separate pieces of paper.
>
> The third day
> We spent the morning clustering the pieces of paper with relevant sentences and ideas onto a large table in order to provide them with a logical framework. This resulted in the following grid:

		us		
In the beginning				
		our parents		
		Discovering this school's ideals		
Now			Our weaknesses	
		Our partial answer		
				By parents
			Pressure	
				By the world

The fourth day
We spent the whole afternoon, i.e. five hours on it. On the basis of the grid that we have produced together, each of us re-wrote the letter following the common framework.

The fifth day
We worked all together and we spent both morning and afternoon on it. Each of us read the respective part of the letter concerning the first topic on the grid. Together we decided what the best text concerning the first topic should be, on the basis of the best individual phrases.
We went on in this way for each of the grid topics.
The final text includes a total of 1,128 words.

The sixth day
The text that was collectively agreed upon the day before was read aloud and copied by each of us in order to ensure that each of us had a copy of it.
The text was written by each of us on the left half-page so that the rest of the afternoon (five hours) each of us can write down on the right half-page any suggestion in order to correct, improve, cut, provide examples and include new concepts to the original text.

The seventh and eighth days
We worked both morning and evening on it.
Sentence by sentence, each of us told the others their respective suggestions.

The ninth day
We worked on it in the morning. We continued to discuss and to accept (or not) the various changes while one of us was writing the final text, the one to be mailed to Vho.

The final text includes a total of 823 words, 305 less than the previous text, although it has been enriched by many new concepts. Milani reports that

> the work of the final three days was met with enthusiasm by me and by the pupils. It was extraordinary at times to see how the younger ones were able to find better solutions compared to those suggested by the older ones. There were few doubts: usually the best solution would quite naturally gain everybody's preference.
>
> In fact, once we had established what we wanted to say it was mainly a matter of finding the best way to say it. Usually this was not a matter for discussion. *Objectively* there is a solution that is better than the others. In this phase we can study together all problems concerning the art of writing and specifically how to complete and how to simplify, i.e., trying to identify what we have not said yet as well as trying to say it with the minimum amount of resources. We also tried to guess the reader's reaction, delete repetitions, the ugly sounds, the adjectives and the minor sentences that are not essential, sentences that are too long. This implies that we ask endlessly to what extent a concept is true, where should it be placed within a logical framework, to what extent is it an essential one, to what extent does the reader have the necessary means to understand it and therefore to what extent it might cause misunderstandings.

We also wanted to avoid sentences that might result in being too choosy. But we told ourselves not to. The art of writing is a matter of being able to express thoroughly who we are and what we think, not to put up a mask and try to look better than what we are. It must be said that for years I have been nurturing the pride of these pupils. When I am face to face with a student or somebody from the city I do my best to humiliate them, to take away from them part of their self-assured feeling. When I am face to face with a peasant or with a worker I am doing the opposite: I am trying to make them more self-confident.

Everything I have been reporting in this letter concerns chapters 3, 4, 5 of the letter. They were written by the older pupils, aged 12–16 years. The two older pupils could not collaborate as they lacked time.

The first two chapters were written in a quicker way and they are not as genuine as the others. The first two chapters saw my collaboration as co-author while during the writing of the others I was a mere *chair*. Next time we will not be able to perform again such a complex and especially complex task. We will limit ourselves to less challenging topics. For example what you might ask ourselves to clarify concerning this letter.

Letter by the Barbiana Pupils to the Piadena Pupils

Barbiana 1/11/1963

Dear pupils,
this letter is divided into five chapters. 6th grade pupils drafted the first two chapters while the older pupils drafted the remaining ones.

Chapter 1: Barbiana

Barbiana lies on the Northern side of the Mount Giovi, 470 metres above sea level.

From up here we can see below us the whole of Mugello, the valley crossed by the Sieve river, a tributary river of the Arno river.

Beyond the Mugello valley we see the Apennine Mountains.

Barbiana is not even a village: it is a church and a bunch of houses out in the woods and in the fields.

Usually mountain places like this one have been abandoned. If our school was not here to prevent our parents from moving, Barbiana would be a desert as well. All in all only 39 souls are still living here.

Our fathers work as peasants or construction workers.

The land is very poor because rains are taking the land away and only stones remain. Water flows away down to the plains. That is why peasants have to eat everything they harvest and they are left with nothing to sell.

The workers' life is hard as well. They have to wake up at five in the morning. They have to travel seven kilometres to catch the train and then they have to travel by train one and a half hours in order to get to Florence where they work as construction workers. They come back home at half past eight in the evening.

Many houses, including our school, are not provided with electricity and water connections.

There was no road. We made it so that a car can go through.

Chapter 2: Our school.

Ours is a private school.

It is situated in two of the rooms in the vicarage plus another two that we use as workshops.

In the winter it's a bit tight but from April to October we do our lessons outside and so there's no lack of space!

Now there are 29 of us. 3 girls and 26 boys.

Only nine pupils come from families who live in the parish of Barbiana.

The other five live with other families because their own families live too far away. The other 15 are from other parishes and go home every day, some on foot, some by bicycle, some by scooter. Some of them come from very far away, like Luciano who has to walk through the wood for almost two hours there and back again. The youngest of us is 11 and the oldest 18.

The younger ones study 6th grade. Seventh and eight vocational grades are also available.

Those who have completed vocational training are studying more foreign languages and mechanical design. The languages that they study are French, English, Spanish, and German. Francuccio would like to be a missionary and therefore is now starting to study Arabic as well.

Our timetable is from 8 in the morning to 7.30 in the evening and we have a short break for lunch. In the morning, before 8.00 those who live nearby usually work at their place, in the stable or cutting wood.

We never have recreational breaks and we don't play games either.

When it snows, after lunch we ski for an hour and during summer time we swim in a small swimming pool that we have built by ourselves.

We consider these activities not as recreational breaks but as very fascinating school subjects! Our teacher wants us to learn them only because they might turn to be useful in our lives.

We have 365 school days, 366 when the year is a bissextile one.

Sundays are different from the other days only because we go to mass.

We have two rooms that we call workshops.

There we learn how to work with wood and iron and we build all the tools we need for our school.

We have 23 teachers! Because each one of us teaches the ones who are younger than us, except for seven, the youngest ones. In order to get our diploma we have to take our final exam in a State school.

Chapter 3: Why did we come to school in the beginning

Before coming to school neither us nor our parents knew what the Barbiana school was.

What we were thinking

We didn't all come for the same reasons.

For those of us living in Barbiana, it was simple:

In the morning we had to go to primary school and in the afternoon we had to work in the fields. We were envious of our older brothers who could spend the whole day at school and therefore were avoiding most jobs in the fields. We were always alone, they were always with their friends.

We like to do what the others do. When everybody is playing we like to play as well; here where everybody is into studying we like to study as well.

For those of us that came from neighbouring places there were different reasons for coming to the school.

Five came against their will (for Arnaldo it was meant as a punishment).

On the contrary, for two of us it was a matter of convincing our parents, as they did not want to let us come to this school (we had been disgusted by our previous school experience).

But the majority came in agreement with our parents.

Five of us came because they were attracted by school subjects of little importance such as skiing or swimming or just to do as some friends were doing.

Eight of us came because either we would go to school or we would have to work. We chose to go to school to work less.

In any case nobody thought of getting a diploma so as to earn more money or work less hard in the future. The idea didn't occur to us spontaneously and if it did occur to some of us, it was only because we were influenced by our parents.

What our parents were thinking

It seems that such thoughts are normal thoughts for parents, judging on the basis of the way our parents think.

The only things that we get to hear from our parents are: "Make sure you pass the exams! When you are going to pass them I'll give you a present! I'll beat you if you fail! Do you want to be a peasant as your father? Look at the job position of those who hold a secondary school degree!."

Listening to them one gets the impression that the only concerns in this world should be ourselves, money, how to make it.

On the one hand it might seem that they are educating us to become selfish. But on the other hand they provide us with plenty of examples of how generous one should be: they are always ready to help other people, the way they care for us is a continuous reminder of the way they can forget about themselves. Often their words are not mirroring their actual thoughts, they just repeat what everybody usually says.

Chapter 4: Why do we come to school now

Slowly we realized that this is a special school: there are no marks, no reports and no risk of failing or having to repeat a year. With all the hours and days we are at school, exams are easy so we can get through the whole year without having to think about them too much. We don't ignore them completely though, because we want to make our parents happy with that piece of paper that they hold in such admiration, otherwise they wouldn't let us come any more.

In any case, at school we have such a wealth of time and we can use it to have in-depth understanding concerning all school subjects and to study new and more fascinating subjects.

This deep, rich school where nobody feels afraid made all of us want to keep coming after just a few days. And that's not all: after a few months each of us was fascinated by knowledge in itself. But we still had one discovery to make: loving knowledge can be selfish too. The prior showed us a higher ideal: to look for knowledge so as to use it for serving others; for example, dedicating our adult lives to teaching or politics or the trade unions or the apostolic life or other such things.

That is why here we often talk of and we stand behind those who are in a weaker position: African people, Asian people, southern people, Italians, workers, peasants, mountain people.

However, the prior says that we cannot do anything in whatever field for the other human beings until we learn how to communicate.

That is why in terms of the amount of time we are investing in the various school subjects languages are the main subject.

In the first place we have to learn Italian otherwise we cannot learn foreign languages. And then we are trying to learn as many languages as possible because we are not alone in this world.

We would like all poor people in the world to study languages in order to understand each other and to be able to organise themselves. In this way there would be no more oppressors, nor homelands, nor wars.

Chapter 5: Intentions are good, but when it comes to facts, it's a different thing altogether

All of us would like to live today and for the rest of our lives in the light of these ideals. But under pressure from our parents, the middle class world and a pinch of our own selfishness, we are all continuously tempted to fall back into only thinking of ourselves.

Our weakness

To give you an example, one of the older pupils—who was already performing extremely well in maths—used to stay up all night to study more maths. Another one of us, after having studied here for seven years went on to enroll in an electrical engineering secondary school.

At times some of us can neglect a discussion to stare at a motorbike as urban kids do. Had we at our disposal even more silly things such as a television or a ball we cannot guarantee that some of us would not be weak enough to waste various half hours with such things.

Pressure by our parents and by the world

Nonetheless we are free to leave the school at any time and to get a job and to spend money as most people do.

You should not believe that if we are not doing so it is because of pressure by our parents. On the contrary. Especially those of us who graduated, we are constantly arguing with our families because they push us to find a job and to make a career.

When we tell our families that we would like to dedicate our lives to serve other human beings they look down at us, even those who call themselves communist.

It is not their fault. It is because even the poor people are immersed in this bourgeois world that puts pressure on them as they are putting pressure on us.

This school has helped us to defend ourselves, yet our poor parents haven't had this or any other kind of schooling.

The Second Letter by the Barbiana Pupils

In "*La parola fa eguali. Il segreto della Scuola di Barbiana*" (The word makes us equal. Barbiana's school secret, 2005), Michele Gesualdi published two letters by Lorenzo Milani dated January 15, 1964, and February 2, 1964, and addressed to teacher Mario Lodi. In the two letters Lorenzo Milani explains that Lodi's pupils are going to receive a collective text to be drafted by Barbiana's pupils in response to the question "Who are the bourgeois people?" He is also explaining that his pupils were finding it difficult to finalize the text. Gesualdi (2005, pp. 142–146) includes the draft text trying to answer the question "Who are the bourgeois people?"

Draft letter by the Barbiana pupils to the Val Piadena pupils concerning the meaning of the word *bourgeois*.

> Dear kids,
>
> Often we are using the word bourgeois. However, trying to explain such a word to you we have become aware that at times the meaning we are attaching to it varies. Therefore it is impossible to provide a simple definition of it....
>
> Once the chaotic barbaric invasion era was over craftsmen were the first to settle again on the plains by crossroads or along a river.... Their group of houses would be called "borgo" (little town) and therefore the "borgo"'s citizens were called "borghesi" ("bourgeois" in French). In the Middle Ages the bourgeois people were those who were neither noble nor peasant. Back then people would use the term bourgeois as we use citizen today.
>
> As time went by the small workshops evolved into the first factories as major trade exchanges evolved from the small shops. In this way the bourgeois people had the opportunity to become wealthier and educated while the feudal hierarchy and their peasants remained isolated and poor. The nobles wanted to keep the privileges that in the past had been granted to them by emperors such as avoiding taxes. The newly rich, the bourgeois people claimed that they wanted to address such inequality. In order to do so, in France the bourgeois people had to cut of the nobles' heads. What they really wanted was to avoid paying taxes themselves and to have only the poor people paying them. They achieved it and until today only poor people pay taxes.
>
> In Italy the revolution involved less blood shedding. Once the Austrians were defeated the bourgeois people entered into an alliance with the nobles and today they are mingled into one single class: in this way there is no more difference between the nobles and the bourgeois people. The only actual divide is between poor and bourgeois people. The whole power is in the hands of the bourgeois people. In the beginning they could keep it for themselves by allowing only rich people to vote. For instance until 1880 only 2% of the population was allowed to vote. Between 1880 and 1909 only 7% of the population was allowed to vote. Today everybody can vote and since the amount of poor people is far larger than rich people in theory poor people should rule. Unfortunately in reality the bourgeois people did not lose their power. They acted in two ways in order to avoid losing it. To begin with they achieved power through violence (the fascist period, 1922–1945). Once

fascism was defeated they found a new way. They based their power upon wealth and education. They have money and they know how to spend it in order to keep the power in their own hands. To this purpose they organised themselves. Many enterprises joined forces to create powerful groups and all together they are united with the employers union, Confindustria. This organisation is so powerful that it is able to sponsor parties, to bribe members of parliament, trade unionists....

However, their major effort goes into negatively affecting the education of poor people so that they are unable to use their two major achievements: voting and striking. To begin with they gained control of most newspapers and they have found a way to control television, cinema and radio.

By controlling all means of communication they are able to spread distorted news and most important they are able to educate people to be indifferent at the political and trade union level. They do so by talking in negative terms of political and trade union commitment as well as of the working class in general, using as rationale religion, anti-communism, or the inter-class idea that we should all love each other, poor and rich people. Moreover, they do so in an indirect way by pushing people to focus on artificial problems that have nothing to do with political commitment such as homeland and borders....

The most direct way by which the bourgeois people affect poor people is through educational policies. To begin with in Italy they have kept an enormous amount of people in a state of illiteracy. Today they are still 5 million. Through the taxes the bourgeois governments have taken the money from the poor people and they have spent it to produce weapons and to send poor people to fight other poor people. And at the end of the wars they spend money to build monuments to those who died during the war while they should be building schools for their children. Even if the 5 million poor people get to vote they will never obtain power. And then we have to take into account that those who are only able to study at primary school level are an enormous amount of people who are not able to defend themselves from commercial adverts etc.

In order to keep as many poor people as possible in such conditions the bourgeois people have also keep unemployment rates at certain level, while leaving salary and social security contributions low enough to limit the number of those who go to school.

The few that can access school are eliminated by the selective school system as school today resembles more a court than a school. Pupils try to obtain grades rather than to learn. Teachers are mainly judging and turning down rather than educating.

Through marks and exams those who made it to the 8th grade are exactly the half of those who entered the 6th grade. Was it necessary to prevent them from studying even during those mere three years? And if they had to eliminate some of them could they not wait until 8th grade? This selective school system has achieved yet another bourgeois objective: conditioning the poor people's children to hate school. Rich people's children also hate school, but they are able to obtain grades since their families pay extra lessons for them. The educational impact of the school lies mainly in the fact that kids get used to trying to get their diploma for their own individual benefit. In addition, the bourgeois people prevented school curricula from addressing issues such as political and trade union commitment. This is why the school today is a school generating selfishness and individualism.

In this way they make sure that nobody is able to compete for power. Poor people have their responsibilities as well. It is not important to add many examples here because for every responsibility of the oppressors there is almost an equal number of responsibilities by the oppressed. Gandhi used to say: "It is not the English guns but rather the deficiencies of the Indians that keep India in slavery." For instance the bourgeois build a stadium in order to make the poor people numb. And yes, what do the poor people do? They run into it as a flock of sheep, they spend their money, they shout and they neglect school, parties and trade unions. So far we have been talking of poor and rich people and maybe some of you have been asking yourselves how does one know whether he or she belongs to one or the other category. When there were slaves the border was clear cut. Today things are more complex. You have to imagine society as a pyramid. At the base of the pyramid there are the illiterate ones. They are oppressed by everybody and they don't oppress anybody. The top of the pyramid is made up of those who are extremely rich and who are ruling: they oppress everybody and they are not oppressed by anybody. Everybody else, probably the vast majority of people, are at the same time oppressed and oppressors. A worker that is appointed as head of his team turns into an oppressor of his fellow workers, although in turn he is oppressed by his boss and so forth.

In this (draft) letter Barbiana's pupils address a crucial topic and the nature of their cultural transition. The importance of properly understanding the evolution of the bourgeois sector from a historical perspective is enhanced by some of the dialogues that intellectuals who were sympathetic with Lorenzo Milani's approach had with the Barbiana's pupils, one example being the opening statement made by Pierpaolo Pasolini (in Gennari, 2008, pp. 138–146) in Milan, at Casa della Cultura, on October 17, 1967, on the occasion of a public discussion with Barbiana's pupils after they had published *Letter to a Teacher*.

Pasolini states that he is impressed by *Letter to a Teacher*:

There is a question that according to me the Barbiana's kids did not ask themselves although they show a unique and honest effort to search for the truth, an effort which is generous and moving and that is unique in Italy. They did not ask themselves what is the nature of the culture of the teacher that they are writing to, i.e., what is bourgeois culture made of and where was it born? Had they formulated this question and had they tried to provide an in-depth answer maybe they would have come to the same answer that I would provide right now. The culture of the teacher, i.e., her petit-bourgeois culture comes from the peasant world. In other words, there is a first historical phase during the industrial period when the bourgeois class of the industrialized countries such as France and England—one hundred years ago—and Italy—twenty years ago—keeps as its own moral standards the moral standards of the pre-industrial world, i.e., of the peasant and crafts world. That is why we keep repeating that the petit-bourgeois culture of the countries that are at the beginning of their industrial phase is a "provincial" culture.... The ideas of the Barbiana's kids are immersed in and given shape by the very same peasant moral frame that later became the petit-bourgeois moral of the teacher that they are addressing themselves to. What I would like to say is that their innovative message, although it comes with violent new contents that make us enthusiastic, at the same time, responds to an old peasant and petit-bourgeois rationale that is making the message lose part of its explosive dimension, it makes it slightly outdated.

I would like to provide three examples of these outdated views....

In the first place, I don't know whether this is intended or not, they continue to consider sexual taboos as the only way to progress. In fact, they suggest to teachers to remain single all their life or for the most part of it—exactly what Mao is asking his citizens....We can no longer consider sexual taboos as the only way for a civilization to progress....While there is a whole peasant nation behind the idealistic and terrorist discipline of Mao's red guards, you are carrying with you just one period of your society, the peasant period. While in China this peasant world is still "the world," in Italy it has been confined....Your revolution, your claims are the product of a provincial world. The specificity of the peasant world remains defined and partial within your discourse. (Pasolini, 2008, pp. 143–144)

Pasolini's words reveal how little the actual educational work at Barbiana was known and understood even by friends and intellectuals who considered themselves close to Barbiana's ideals and pedagogy. As we know, not only did Barbiana's pupils ask themselves the question "What is bourgeois culture made of and where was it born?," they produced a collective text on it while keeping such a question open. It is remarkable that while underestimating the depth of the collective and cultural work being carried out at the Barbiana school, Pasolini senses a core problem for Barbiana's pupils, a problem that concerns the core of their cultural work and that Jerome Bruner (1991) would describe as a matter of "hermeneutic composability."

A preliminary word of explanation is needed here. The word hermeneutic implies that there is a text or a text analogue through which somebody has been trying to express a meaning and from which somebody is trying to extract a meaning. This in turn implies that there is a difference between what is expressed in the text and what the text might mean, and furthermore that there is no unique solution to the task of determining the meaning for this expression. Such hermeneutic interpretation is required when there is neither a rational method of assuring the "truth" of a meaning assigned to the text as a whole, nor an empirical method for determining the verifiability of the constituent elements that make up the text. In effect, the best hope of hermeneutic analysis is to provide an intuitively convincing account of the meaning of the text as a whole in the light of the constituent parts that make it up. This leads to the dilemma of the so-called hermeneutic circle—in which we try to justify the "rightness" of one reading of a text in terms of other readings rather than by, say, rational deduction or empirical proof. The most concrete way of explicating this dilemma or "circle" is The Narrative Construction of Reality by reference to the relations between the meanings assigned the whole of a text (say a story) and its constituent parts. As Charles Taylor puts it, "we are trying to establish a reading for the whole text, and for this we appeal to readings of its partial expressions; and yet because we are dealing with meaning, with making-sense, where expressions only make sense or not in relation to others, the readings of partial expressions depend on those of others, and ultimately of the whole. (p. 8)

In the accompanying letter to the first letter written by the Barbiana pupils to Mario Lodi's pupils, Lorenzo Milani (F. Gesualdi and Corzo Toral, 1992, p. 18) wrote:

> As we were motivated to achieve as much precision in the way we express ourselves as possible…we witnessed something funny, unforeseen. Thinking about it afterwards we can explain it very well. Collaboration and deep reflection have produced a letter that although being of the exclusive authorships of these pupils—the older ones not having a more important role compared to the younger ones—it ends up revealing a position that is much more mature than the position of any of its single authors.
>
> I would explain it in the following way: each pupil knows a very limited number of words that he or she would use as well as a huge number of words that he or she would understand very well. Concerning these latter words they are very able to assess their qualities. Nonetheless these are not words that would come easily to their mind.
>
> When we read aloud 25 individually written texts it is always the case that one or the other pupil, not necessarily the older ones, is providing a word or phrase that is especially right or straight to the point. All those who are listening to him or her—although they were not able to find such a word or phrase at the time of writing their respective texts—get the sudden insight that this word or phrase is the most appropriate one and they request it to be adopted in the common text. This is why the common text acquired such a rhythm and such an adult pace (I would dare to say that it acquired the pace of an adult that is considering his or her own words!, a very rare case indeed). In other words this text meets their ears' cultural level, not their pens' or mouths' cultural level.

While Barbiana's pupils felt they had accomplished their goals in their first letter to Mario Lodi's pupils, the question about their understanding of the "bourgeois" concept (a term frequently used in their first letter) was considered by them to be more problematic. It was not the only case. M. Gesualdi (2005, pp. 147–148) published another draft collective text, which was also not finalized. It was meant as a response to a letter asking Lorenzo Milani whether his idea that obedience was no longer a virtue applied only to citizen-State relations or to sons/daughters–parents relations as well. It seems that in both cases the problems the Barbiana kids were facing concerned hermeneutic composability as well as challenges concerning what Jerome Bruner (1991) defines as context sensitivity and negotiability.

This is a topic whose complexities we have already visited in an earlier discussion of "hermeneutic composability" and the interpretability of narrative. In considering context, the familiar issues of narrative intention and background knowledge arise again. With respect to the first of these, most literary theory has abandoned Coleridge's dictum that the reader should suspend disbelief and stand, as it were, naked before the text. Today we have reader-response theory and books with titles such as *Prospecting: From Reader Response to Literary Anthropology* (Iser, 1989). Indeed, the prevailing view is that the notion of suspending disbelief is at best an idealization of the reader and at worst a distortion of what the process of narrative comprehension involves. Inevitably, we assimilate narrative on our own terms, however much (in Wolfgang Iser's account) we treat the occasion of a narrative recital as a specialized speech act (Iser, 1974). We inevitably take the teller's intentions into account and do so in terms of our background knowledge (and, indeed, in the light of our presuppositions about the teller's background knowledge).

We have a strong hunch, which may at first seem counterintuitive, that it is this context sensitivity that makes narrative discourse in everyday life such a viable instrument for cultural negotiation. You tell your version; I tell mine, and we rarely need legal confrontation to settle the difference. Principles of charity and presumptions of relevance are balanced against principles of sufficient ignorance and sufficient doubt to a degree one would not expect where criteria of consistency and verification prevailed.

We seem to be able to take competing versions of a story with a perspectival grain of salt, much more so than in the case of arguments or proofs. Judy Dunn's remarkable book on the beginning of social understanding in children makes it plain that this type of negotiation of different narrative versions starts early and is deeply imbedded in such practical social actions as the offering of excuses, not merely in storytelling per se (Dunn, 1988). I think it is precisely this interplay of perspectives in arriving at "narrative truth" that has led philosophers like Richard Rorty (1979) to abandon univocally verificationist views of truth in favor of pragmatic ones (Taylor, 1989). Nor is it surprising that anthropologists have increasingly turned away from positivist descriptions of cultures toward an interpretive one in which not objective categories but "meanings" are sought for, not meanings imposed *ex hypothesi* by an outsider, the anthropologist, but ones arrived at by indigenous participants immersed in the culture's own processes for negotiating meaning (see, for example, Geertz's [1983] essay on "thick interpretation").

Steps to a Collective Approach to Writing

According to Gesualdi (F. Gesualdi and Corzo Toral, 1992, p. 21) Lorenzo Milani was concerned with "educating without transmitting the defects of the bourgeois world, two of them being talking to please oneself and writing to show off one's knowledge."

Lorenzo Milani provided his pupils with a critical literacy framework and a social environment where each participant could feel safe to take risks because school was no longer a matter of controlling and evaluating knowledge; rather, it encouraged individuals to take responsibility for their own learning and for their peers' learning. Together they sought to understand and to apply their knowledge in ways that could make a difference in the world they lived in.

Their collective writing illustrates the effort to achieve social change agency. This type of transformative and participatory practice encourages persons to support and to be involved in political change and to make an impact on the context in which one lives. As authors such as Smith (2003) and Williams (2012) outline, both the concept and context of reading imply a communal structure that impinges on the act itself. Reading in turn re-addresses this structure in a continuous process of intellectual, social, and dynamic interaction that brings about positive change with the understanding that the world can be shaped by individuals in a collective effort.

As stated by Freire (1994):

> To acquire literacy is more than to psychologically and mechanically dominate reading and writing techniques. It is to dominate these techniques in terms of consciousness; to understand what one reads and to write what one understands; it is to communicate graphically. Acquiring literacy does not involve memorizing sentences, words, or syllables, lifeless objects unconnected to an existential universe but rather an attitude of creation and re-creation, a self-transformation producing a stance of intervention in one's context. (p. 48)

Collective writing was a response to such preoccupations but an even deeper concern, for Lorenzo Milani, was to avoid being framed as somebody practicing a specific method or having a pedagogical model. At the core of his educational activity was the choice of *being with* the students that lived in and/or attended the Barbiana school. Any model or framed method would have prevented him from the necessary active listening and adopting the "ignorant" attitude that was needed to root learning within their cultural environment.

Nonetheless, there have been several attempts to provide methodological accounts of his way of approaching collective writing.

According to Sidoti (2002) the Barbiana collective writing approach can be framed according to four main phases:

- Collecting ideas
- Identifying key issues (or planning)
- Drafting
- Rereading (reviewing)

F. Gesualdi and Corzo Toral (1992, pp. 47–86) provide examples of further use of the collective writing approach and summarize it in eight steps:

Step 1: Choosing the theme and the reader
Step 2: Collecting ideas
Step 3: Clustering ideas according to chapters and paragraphs
Step 4: Organizing ideas within chapters and paragraphs
Step 5: Writing the full text
Step 6: General revision of the full text
Step 7: Simplifying and improving the full text
Step 8: Revision of the full text by external actors

Step 1: Choosing the Theme and the Reader

Collective writing should be based on something important and useful to communicate, not necessarily something "new." To understand how to communicate, the group needs to identify to whom the text is being addressed, even when it is a matter of an imaginary (individual or group) receiver. This means that the letter format is not always the most suitable one.

Step 2: Collecting Ideas

This phase should have the features of a brainstorming activity welcoming all ideas: positive ideas, negative ideas, short comments, short narratives, opinions.

It is helpful for the follow-up work to write down each contribution on a separate piece of paper to enable those who want to read them to handle them one by one.

Corzo Toral lists three different ways to approach the collection of ideas.

Participants can be encouraged to reflect on the topic on their own. This can last various days. It is useful to suggest that they have a notebook to note their ideas.

A second way to tackle the collection of ideas is to encourage participants to produce individual texts: letters, essays, etc. They can then select and copy single ideas onto separate pieces of paper.

A third way to initiate the process is to facilitate a conversation among the members of the group while somebody is noting on a flip-chart the various ideas and areas of disagreement. Again, once the activity is over, it is a matter of selecting and copying individual ideas onto separate pieces of paper.

Step 3: Clustering Ideas According to Chapters and Paragraphs

In this phase the group concentrates on grouping ideas that have similar contents. The process generates chapters and the initial structure of the text. It is important in this phase to value diversity and avoid being too quick in judging that two ideas are the same. A sentence might repeat most of what another sentence says, but it might bear a new element as well.

Step 4: Organizing Ideas within Chapters and Paragraphs

F. Gesualdi and Corzo Toral (1992, p. 56) provide four key ideas concerning this purpose:

1. To organize key ideas according to a logical framework;
2. To link them by using new words and at the same time respecting contradictions;
3. To eliminate repetitions; and
4. To streamline tense and subjects so that verbs are used in a consistent way and the text appears to the reader as having a collective single voice.

From a practical perspective they suggest three approaches concerning this step:

1. A group comprising no more than seven participants is suited to sit around a table on which they place the various pieces of paper and organize them according to their positions.
2. In cases when the participants are more than seven and are familiar enough with the logical framework, it is usually easier to form subgroups and to assign different paragraphs to different groups.
3. In cases when the participants are numerous and not familiar with the logical framework, it is important to work in plenary sessions and to ensure that each participant has a copy of the sentences in front of him or her. As the sentences can be rewritten, it can be useful to have the sentences copied on the left side of a sheet of paper to allow each participant to write, on the right side, the results of the collective discussion.

Step 5: Writing the Full Text

On the basis of the previous work the participants proceed to draft a first version of the text by ordering the paragraphs in a logical sequence. This phase of the work can be facilitated by writing on a flip-chart the title of the chapters and within each chapter the titles of the various paragraphs. This session needs a chair to facilitate the discussion and to question the rationale behind each suggestion.

Step 6: General Revision of the Full Text

Once the text is drafted it is a matter of checking whether it is well organized, whether it expresses all the various aspects that have been mentioned during the work, and whether it is clear, readable, and effective.

Check whether the text is providing too much attention to marginal issues rather than to core issues, whether there are repetitions, whether the text has general consistency or certain sentences should be better moved elsewhere to ensure enhanced coherence and effectiveness.

At the beginning of the process it is worth stating again to the whole group why the text is being written and to allow enough time to all participants to reread the text and write individual comments on their own copies.

Step 7: Simplifying and Improving the Full Text

At this stage the text is being checked in detail to delete any sentence that is not fully convincing and whenever possible to choose words that can be understood by everybody.

Again the full text is usually provided to each participant. It is copied onto the left side of the page to allow for individual reading, with comments on the right side of the page. Comments are then shared and the text is finalized during a plenary session.

Step 8: Revision of the Full Text by External Actors

The draft version of the text is provided to many people, preferably those with minimal schooling for them to read the text and to share with the authors their feelings concerning the different parts of the text. Usually a letter is tested with both people who have had only a few years of schooling and potential final readers and friends. Their comments help the writers in further understanding and clarifying the final version of the text.

As with Paulo Freire, Lorenzo Milani would always reject the idea of designing a pedagogical model or methodology on the grounds that those who are responsible for an educational process should "be" with those who are learning rather than "have" a model. Nevertheless, the outline of the collective writing approach, as developed at Barbiana and described by F. Gesualdi and Corzo Toral (1992), provides significant evidence of the importance that Lorenzo Milani attributed to creating the proper conditions for problematizing the content at the core of the learning process. The same concern is expressed by Gianni Rodari (1973/2001, pp. 182–183).

In his best-known pedagogical book, Rodari grounds the same concerns in the scholarly writings of Jerome S. Bruner. In *On Knowing—Essays for the Left Hand*, Bruner (1964) goes back to the English philosopher T.D. Weldon, who describes problem-solving in "an interesting and picturesque way" (pp. 93–94). According to Weldon, we are in the best position to solve a problem when we are able to turn it into a riddle. In this way we transform a difficulty into something that we are able to work on. This is why many of our "discoveries" are based on the ability to find the appropriate form to work on something that is challenging.

Lorenzo Milani saw in this ability a key challenge for structuring an effective learning process and considered affective collective writing a form of art, that is, of producing accuracy and precision in a collective way.

These aspects of the learning activities at the Barbiana school are reflected in some of Lorenzo Milani's letters. There is the letter dated November 3, 1963, that Lorenzo Milani writes to teacher Mario Lodi and his pupils to accompany the collective letter mailed by the Barbiana pupils. As previously mentioned, he stresses that "In all these years I have been teaching I have never had such a complete and great opportunity to study in depth the art of writing with my students. So everything is fine for us. I'm even very enthusiastic about it." Gesualdi and Corzo Toral (2008, p. 342) highlight that in this accompanying letter, Milani links the idea of "art" to the idea of "truth," something that had already happened at the occasion of the "Letter to don Piero," which is close to the St. John's Gospel (8, 32): "Truth will make you free." Corzo Toral shares with Milani the idea that collective writing is not just a matter of "writing the truth" but rather a means to uncover the truth by writing. According to Lorenzo Milani (as quoted by Coccia, 1967), "A masterpiece means a text or a painting that is able to convey the thought, to communicate deeply."

Such aspects of learning at Barbiana are also reflected in the writings of the people who shared that experience with him and the Barbiana students.

In *Non so se don Lorenzo* (I don't know whether Don Lorenzo...), Adele Corradi (2012) recalls some of the key moments of her life at the Barbiana school. She writes:

> It seems to me that it was the pupils who provided the style of the "Letter to a Teacher." Of course none of them would have been able to write in that way without the help of the others. And some ideas would have not occurred to Don Lorenzo without talking to the pupils, without listening to them, without confessing them, without discussing with them. When one takes into account all this, I agree with Aldo when in his Manifesto he lists some twenty authors of the "Letter to a Teacher." I think forty or even one hundred could be listed. This is why it is right that we don't know the names of those eight pupils

who worked on that text every morning for nine months. They were the first ones to think that this way is right. Those eight names could have been on the book cover. None of them asked to do so. None of them thought about it. Forty years later none of those eight boys talked about their long and patient work. Their silence is very eloquent: the author of the "Letter to a Teacher" is the Barbiana school. (p. 133)

Herself a teacher, Corradi recalls that "Don Milani never gave me any advice on how to teach in the school where I was teaching, except concerning collective writing. But I was not brave enough. I only dared to use it years after he passed away. I became passionate about it because in this way pupils were participating. In the afternoon pupils would always suggest to me that we have collective writing."[2]

Collective Writing as Critical Literacy Practice

Along with the teachers such as Bernardini (1968) and Lodi, and with educators and writers such as Rodari, Lorenzo Milani and the Barbiana pupils contributed to critical literacy both as a practical approach and as a deep analysis of dominant Italian and capitalist cultural structures. Later, within the Italian school Mario Lodi was able to merge in a coherent learning manner his experience with collective local inquiry and printed media, Rodari's ability to find and to put to use a generative and creative initial input, and Barbiana's structured dialogue and planning resources.

The collective writing of the Barbiana students is especially effective in responding to the four key dimensions of critical literacy practices as identified by authors such as Van Sluys (Van Sluys, Lewison, and Seely Flint, 2006): "Critical literacy practices are often described as the taking up of alternative reading positions, questioning how texts work ideologically (Muspratt, Luke, & Freebody, 1997), engaging in the tensions of competing voices (Edelsky, 1999), moving toward the critique of issues that surround us (P. Green, 2001), and transforming social conditions (Freire & Macedo, 1987, p. 199)."

Their collective writing practice is also a practice of encouraging

> social cultural and linguistic transformation through inquiry, analysis and response to issues of power, justice, and equity among others. This is achieved by creating a social acuity in students through various pedagogical practices as related to literacy learning. Literacy learning in this context goes much more beyond the mere decoding of words but their inherent meaning and use with a social framework. This concept creates authentic avenues for conscious interrogations of the social framework and the world of the words as they relate to the student.…Literacy learning, as participatory democratic practices, is about empowering individuals to enable social change and positively impact the environment that surrounds them. Both the concept and context of literacy imply a communal structure that

impinges on the act itself. Literacy in turn re-addresses this structure in a continuous intellectual, social and dynamic interaction that effects positive change with the understanding that the world can be shaped by individuals in a collective effort. (Williams, 2012)

After Lorenzo Milani passed away, Ernesto Balducci was instrumental, in his writings, in explaining how much his work and his ideas were too far ahead of his (and our) time. Like Paulo Freire, Lorenzo Milani is "out of his time" because he is radically democratic. It becomes increasingly difficult to understand Milani's educational approach at a time dominated by a "minimal" idea of democracy, that is, democracy as an appendix to the neoliberal economic approach.

Milani's educational approach is concerned with "process" while the neoliberal economic approach is concerned with the "product." And it is concerned with the extent to which such a product can be commodified. Milani's concern connects with his initial idea of the school: on May 2, 1955, when considering the idea of setting up a popular education center in Firenze, Milani writes to his friend Gian Paolo Meucci stating that the proposed "school" should be named after Socrates. His concern is still an urgent one, similar to the critical pedagogy concerns of the likes of Freire. Ernesto Balducci (2002) knew Milani well. He has been among the first ones to link Milani's and Freire's works: while Milani used to say that a group of 27 kids is also a group of 27 masters and that teaching is a circular activity, Freire would translate such views into the idea that nobody educates anybody because people educate each other.

In different ways, both Milani and Freire were able to practice disobedience; in the first place such disobedience concerns the logic of violence and of weapons. And both oriented their pedagogical work toward the art of dialogue. Both are providing us with concrete ways to reflect on a cultural, communicative, and transformative process on the basis of the human capacity to say NO, in collective ways, to violent structures. In Milani's words, there are times when obedience is no longer a virtue!

Notes

Chapter 1

1. Retrieved from http://www.freireproject.org/content/freire-international-project-critical-pedagogy.

Chapter 2

1. The initiative was termed the "Aventine Secession" in memory of the Plebian protest against the Patricians in Ancient Rome.
2. Chemist, poet, philosopher, proficient linguist in six different languages, Lorenzo's father was a true intellectual. Lorenzo also had an older brother Adriano and a younger sister Elena. His great-grandfather, Domenico Comparetti, was one of the most famous Italian humanists and a well-known linguist in as many as 19 languages, while his grandfather was a well-known archaeologist.
3. His grandmother on his mother's side was a friend of Italo Svevo, one of the most important Italian writers and novelists of the last century.
4. He was never a model student. He failed his last year of junior high school and was made to resit his exams, having obtained just 3/10 in Italian and 4/10 in Latin. After the family crisis brought on by his lack of success at school he managed to pass his resits but he failed to improve in the first year of senior high school. Incredibly he then decided, as recounted in the text, to skip a year and put his name forward for

the entrance exams to the last year of senior high as a private candidate and succeeded in passing them, moving directly on to the final year. When he turned up to sit the exams his Italian teacher commented, "You've got a nerve to try skipping a year after a first year like yours!"

The amazement and surprise that Lorenzo excited in his family during this period were increased when he asked to take Holy Communion during the summer holidays while still at junior high.

5. "Professor Giorgio Pasquali brought him to my studio in via dei Serragli in Florence. Pasquali was a well known man who honored me with his friendship. We had even been out walking together on Mount Morello. He was curious about me, perhaps because I was German and he spoke German too. He knew my painting and knew that I was a teacher so he offered me real proof of his trust by bringing his friend's son to me as a student. He introduced me to Lorenzo Milani who was a handsome, slender boy, friendly, polite and spontaneous with the typical air of a young man from a middle class family. Pasquali explained that he was the son of a very dear friend and grandson of Comparetti, the great Italian humanist. He added that the boy had expressed the desire to become a painter straight after finishing school, to the great surprise of his parents who had never heard him mention anything of the kind before. I discovered that my student was completely unprepared. It was I who made him do the first real drawing of his life. I realized immediately that he was a gifted young man, so instead of simply correcting his drawings I explained how to begin. I told him about simplification and the unity that must be at the basis of every piece of work, drawing or painting. He grasped these ideas immediately and threw himself into his work with real commitment, attempting to put what I had taught him into practice with striking enthusiasm. I had never seen such passion in a school boy." Interview with Hans Joachim Staude by Neera Fallaci in N. Fallaci, 1993, pp. 47–48.

6. He wrote to his mother on March 27, 1944, apologizing for not being able to attend a family celebration because of the spiritual exercises necessary before receiving tonsure: "Has it ever occurred to you that by binding myself to the Lord I am also binding myself to my mother? I will have no other family but yours. If only you knew how much more seminarians love their mothers than those on the outside. I wish you would do all you can to come and to read the liturgy so you can see how beautiful it is."

7. The explicit references in his letters to his mother refer to the "hostile people" who embittered his last two years at the Seminary, or his bitterly ironic reference to the rector before the first lesson he was due to give to the new seminarians on Mass: "the Rector insisted on hearing the whole thing in his study and forbid me from adding even a single word. As well as other important measures of P.S. [public security Ed.] to prevent my first lesson in the seminary from causing serious disturbance to public order."

8. He held the same independent opinion later with his sister. Elena wrote to him to

tell him of her intention to marry Erseo Polacco, lecturer in physics at the University of Pisa, in a civil ceremony at the registry office: "Dear Elena, I am delighted that you are getting married and there is no reason why I should wonder or suffer because you are going to have a civil wedding. Being religious or Christian is a fortune not a duty. I might be sad that you haven't had the fortune to be religious, but not that you are doing something in harmony with what you believe."

9. This is the second reference, in his letters to his mother, to his interest in teaching and his explicit intention to set up a Popular mixed school (although the Popular school at San Donato was for boys only). In a letter dated June 1949 Lorenzo wrote to his mother about his intention to buy a Treccani encyclopedia: "I'm going to get it so that I can put it into the hands of the young, so that they can do what they did with the two Melzi and the two atlases and all those other beautiful books. The whole idea is to produce more educated men who as such will have more educated children or grandchildren who will own a parish library and will know how to look after it with cleanliness and decorum."

10. Saverio Tutino was a famous Italian journalist and long-term foreign correspondent for the newspaper *l'Unità*, first from Paris and then from Cuba. He is founder of the Diary Archives at Pieve Santo Stefano (Arezzo).

11. Almost all of the Italian Popular Party's exponents took refuge in exile. From his own exile in London Don Sturzo continued plotting for the establishment of a Catholic party.

12. The Christian Democrat Party was an active political party from 1942 to 1994. From 1944 to 1994 members of the party were always represented in the Italian Council of Ministers, and in the majority of cases the prime minister (the highest political position in the Italian government) also belonged to the party.

13. These were the years in which numerous Italians devoted themselves to the "black market" as a way of making a living, that is, they illegally bought and sold goods (particularly foodstuff) that were legally forbidden. Hundreds of girls also went into prostitution to serve the Allied military population.

14. Women had actually already voted in the earlier local elections.

15. On March 12, 1947, President of the United States Harry Truman announced to Congress the policy that would take his name, according to which the United States "had the right" to intervene in any part of the world to defeat the "red threat." Just two days earlier the American ambassador to Rome had sent a telegram advising the Department of State that the CIA archives in Rome held the names and contacts of more than 2,000 extreme right wingers who had offered their services to defeat communism. The telegram specified that these men were capable of killing, planting bombs, setting off fires, and spreading propaganda.

16. In 1959 Luigi Einaudi wrote a long letter to Don Milani after having read *Pastoral Experiences*, complimenting him for the book that he greatly appreciated.

17. Just a few years later, Dossetti was to withdraw from politics to become a priest.

18. Increase in production led to the exponential growth of Italian wealth (in just a few years growth increased more than during the whole of the previous century), the car industry was the leading sector (with the huge growth of Fiat, already a mammoth industry) alongside the birth of small- and medium-sized businesses in sectors such as furniture, clothing, household appliances, and shoes. The economic miracle was also made possible thanks to the policy of low wages, which made production costs competitive and allowed Italian industries to increase exportation levels considerably.
19. As Salvadori points out, "The PCI, the PSI up until 1956 and the trade unions controlled by the communists constituted a sort of anti-society or anti-State that placed itself in opposition to society and the Bourgeois State, whose rules they respected and made use of temporarily, while waiting to change them not just radically, and this is the point to keep in mind, but irreversibly (the reverse process, from the superior socio-economic conditions now reached to anything inferior, was unthinkable). The elections were therefore considered preparatory to a definitive transformation, at once social, political, ethical and cultural, whose final aim was that of socialism: a turning point in the system."
20. The costs of setting up and managing the school were the following: one pot of black paint to make a blackboard out of some old planks of wood, 100 lira; one packet to make up one flask of ink, 30 lira; the chalk was given to the school by a pupil who worked in a warehouse; the children brought their own exercise books and pens and this was the only cost they had to incur (Milani, 1957, p. 234).
21. Although he was a teacher, and perhaps more teacher than priest, Don Milani never forgot that he was a priest.
22. An exception can be found in the work of Antonio Gramsci, who voiced his opposition to a totalitarian, state vision of education.
23. In 1923 new programs had been introduced into the Italian primary school by the then director general of the Ministry for Primary Education, Giuseppe Lombardo-Radice. These programs introduce the idea of the centrality of linguistic education, based on respect for the personality of the child (the child's world and values) and his or her dialectic linguistic heritage. With the onset of fascism, Gentile, with whom Lombardo Radice was in good relations, initially defended the developments introduced by the enlightened, liberal pedagogue Lombardo Radice. Later, though, ideological control was exerted through the introduction of the obligatory single text. This process was consolidated further by recourse to standardized teaching practices (even though the concept of "freedom of teaching" remained part of the reform introduced by the same Gentile).
24. On January 7, 1929, a law was to impose a single state text for elementary schools, thus ending the progress made in educational publishing thanks to Lombardo Radice's reforms. The Sicilian educationalist had collaborated with Gentile on the 1923 reform but was later to distance himself from fascism, quickly and definitively, writing to the same Gentile that "after a series of extremely serious yet inconspicuous blows" to his

reform "the decree that introduced the centrally imposed single text for all was the last straw." The Lateran Treaty, sealed on February 11, 1929, allowed the Fascist state to strengthen its position, procuring consensus from the Catholic authorities through "some substantial concessions in the field of education" (Corbi and Sarracino, 1999, p. 65). The treaty declares that Italy is committed to considering the teaching of Christian doctrine according to Catholic tradition, as the foundation and crowning aim of public education. With the treaty religious education was extended from elementary school to all secondary schools. The Catholic Church was awarded the right to select religious education teachers and textbooks (a privilege that still exists today). In the second half of the 1930s a series of provisions aimed to favor private schools (almost all of them exclusively Catholic) that, thanks to their legal recognition, achieved an incredibly high number of enrollments just before the 1940s, equal to 22% of all enrollments.

25. It is worth pointing out that the choice of a Catholic education minister was not the result of mediation but a precise political choice made by De Gasperi, "intended to strengthen ties with the ecclesiastical authorities and win over any remaining dissidents by accommodating the denominational approach to problems related to schooling and education" (Corbi and Sarracino, 1999, pp. 71–72).

26. Article 3 of the decree of the Bishops of Tuscany reads: "For serious moral duty voters must vote for those candidates or list of candidates that know how to defend the rights of God, the Church and the Christian Family." Article 4 reads: "It is warned that the parties who oppose our holy religion also want to: a) remove religious education from school; b) promote so-called civil marriage; c) introduce divorce in Italy." In the electoral roll for the Christian Democrats there were also liberals and social democrats and so Don Milani, mindful of the "betrayal" of April 18, 1948, invited people to vote only for the Christian Democrat candidates and among these, for those who demonstrated a high level of social awareness. Although they weren't Catholic, it seems that the two Freemason candidates (one liberal and one a Marxist democrat) were the ones who made sure that Don Milani was silenced by the Curia.

27. La Pira was mayor of Florence in this period. He was an extraordinary, atypical political figure who paid great attention to social problems and who led a totally sober personal life (renouncing any kind of comfort or privilege). La Pira was to strongly influence the historical period and not just on a local level. Through his friend Meucci, Don Milani tried to organize for him a secret visit to San Donato so as to encourage his pupils. After Dossetti's withdrawal from politics, La Pira became a major exponent of left-wing Christian Democracy.

28. These sledges were a kind of mountain cart that had poles instead of wheels to get over the uneven ground. In Tuscany they were pulled by oxen.

29. He is referring to Beethoven's VII symphony which he had worked on at San Donato. Elena is his sister.

30. Drawn up on the basis of the proposals made by the National School Review, set up by the previous minister Gonnella, and headed by Giovanni Calò.

31. In earlier years there had been a well-known controversy between two conflicting positions within the Christian Democrat Party: future minister Gonnella had talked about the supplementary function of the state school system, while education for him was above all the prerogative of the private sector (where for private he obviously means denominational Catholic schools); Aldo Moro, on the other hand, talked of "integration." In his report to the First Under Commission of the Constituent Assembly, which had the responsibility of defining, among other things, constitutional principles regarding education and culture, Aldo Moro declared that it was wrong to speak "as some do about the supplementary role of the State with regard to education, as if it should only concern itself with education in order to provide for those areas that private schooling cannot reach. NO. The State must surely have an educating role due to its moral prestige, when it knows how to earn it. The state does not supplement but integrates private initiatives, just as private initiatives are integrated with public ones" (in Acts of the Commission for the Constitution, vol. II [1947], Reports and proposals, pp. 48–49).
32. Ovide Decroly (1871–1932) and John Dewey (1859–1952) can be considered the founders of pedagogical activism. The first proposed the observation of the child whose relationship with reality is driven by vital interests, deriving from this the idea of a global method that takes into account the lack of superior mental functions (analysis and synthesis) that are to be developed later. The second insisted specifically on the active and conscious participation of the child within his or her process of development. Activism's key principles can be summarized as child centered (the child plays an active role in the educational process); the value of hands-on learning; motivation (everything the child learns must be linked to the emotional, practical, and cognitive needs of the child); an attention to the environment (the child receives stimulus from the environment); the importance of socialization (a primary need that should be favored and stimulated); anti-authoritarianism (this was particularly innovative in comparison to the past when the adult directed everything in relation to his or her intellectual and mental superiority); anti-intellectualism and the resulting devaluation of programs centered on and determined entirely by cultural knowledge, in the direction of a more free organization of a child's learning (Cambi, 1995).
33. Priming is a specific authorization given to ecclesiastical staff by the Church for the publication of a volume. In Don Milani's case the ecclesiastic proofreader was Father Reginald Santilli, a Dominican who taught sociology in the seminary at the time when Don Milani was still a seminarian.
34. The photographer who came to visit is invited to teach the children how to take and develop photos; the wood carver is invited to teach them how to work with wood; a visiting magician would be invited to do a show; someone who knew about astronomy would be asked to talk about the stars. All visitors had some kind of interest that could be used in school.

35. Don Milani said about Adele Corradi: "Everything that happened at Barbiana was part of the school and was a chance to teach something...anyone who is born into a cultured family receives culture even when they are not at school, while anyone who is born into an illiterate family falls back into illiteracy when they come out of school....There were never lessons when one person talked and the others listened; there was always a work group, a research project and everyone intervened when they were curious or when they didn't understand anything" (Becchi, 2004, pp. 256–258).
36. This quote is only one example; there were numerous references to work, improvements, completion of classrooms, bits of the vicarage, and the building of educational tools of one kind or another.
37. The first day everyone wrote on their own, the second day all the letters were read aloud and everyone noted down the best expressions, the nicest sentences, and the ideas that best matched each person's ideas. The next morning everyone ordered their pieces of paper and notes according to a general framework, and on the fourth day everyone set out to rewrite their letter following the framework that had been agreed together. On the fifth day each person read what they had written about the first point, then the second point, and so on through the seven points that are part of the framework. Out of this a collective work was born that was dictated and written down on the sixth day by each pupil on a piece of paper divided into two columns (the second column was used for each person to write down their cuts, corrections, additions, simplifications, ideas, important omissions, and so on). On the seventh and eighth days the text was examined rigorously: each pupil expressed concerns and corrections for every sentence. The final text, that was much more synthetic than the first, was however clearer and satisfied the pupils better. Don Milani then wrote a long preface describing how the letter was written (Milani, 2007, pp. 207–211).
38. There are a number of references to these threats: "I'm feeling worse than usual and at night we're a bit afraid because every day we receive letters with anonymous fascist threats in them" (Milani, 2007, p. 252).

Chapter 3

1. We are indebted to Professor Roger Dale of the Universities of Bristol and Auckland for this information. Its North American version was therefore produced during the same year that saw the publication in English of Paulo Freire's *Pedagogy of the Oppressed*.
2. See Schugurensky's website titled History of Education: Selected Moments of the 20th Century at http://schugurensky.faculty.asu.edu/moments/1967barbiana.html
3. Translation by one of us from the original in Italian. Retrieved from http://www.chille.it/progetti-in-corso/progetto-don-milani-lettera-a-una-professoressa/
4. Notes on the poor education of a willing educator.

5. The term *Catcom*, short for *Cattolico* (Catholic) and *Communista* (Communist), is a popular term in Italy.
6. Edoardo Martinelli disclosed this in Borg and Mayo, 2007, p. 115, though he mentions *Quaderni del Carcere* (The Prison Notebooks) when making the same point in his book; Martinelli, 2007, p. 8.
7. See Italian original in Milani, 1991, p. 18.
8. Scuola di Barbiana, 1996, p. 92.
9. Scuola di Barbiana, 1996, p. 113.
10. We have seen, in the previous chapter, that while there was a popular outcry when Lorenzo was removed by the Curia from Calenzano, with signed petitions, Lorenzo accepted his fate, trusting in God's "grand design," despite knowing only too well that he was exiled for his search for truth and justice (M. Gesualdi, 2011, pp. 12, 13). God's design was metaphorically conceived as that of an artist's huge canvas—no one had the right to take the brush from the Omnipotent Artist's hands and add one's little detail to the canvas.
11. Lazzarin, 2007, p. 79, in Abbate, 2008, p. 82, writes about kicks up the backside—*pedate sul sedere*.
12. See original in Milani, 1991, p. 31.
13. Italian original in Milani, 1991, p. 12.
14. Original in Italian in Milani, 1991, p. 4.
15. Scuola di Barbiana, 1996, pp. 63, 64.
16. Scuola di Barbiana, 1996, p. 33.
17. Scuola di Barbiana, 1996, p. 68.
18. Scuola di Barbiana, 1996, p. 68.
19. Scuola di Barbiana, 1996, p. 68.
20. Scuola di Barbiana, 1996, p. 19.
21. Scuola di Barbiana, 1996, p. 11.
22. Original reads: "Sbagliano domanda, non dovrebbero preoccuparsi di come *bisogna fare per fare scuola,* ma solo di *come bisogna essere* per poter far scuola."
23. Electronic interview with Edoardo Martinelli in Borg and Mayo, 2007.
24. Scuola di Barbiana, 1996, p. 17.
25. Scuola di Barbiana, 1996, p. 17.
26. Scuola di Barbiana, 1996, p. 29.
27. Scuola di Barbiana, 1996, p. 12.
28. Original reads: "Devo tutto quello che so ai giovani operai e contadini cui ho fatto scuola. Quello che loro credevano di stare imparando da me, son io che l'ho imparato da loro. Io ho insegnato loro soltanto a esprimersi mentre loro mi hanno insegnato a vivere. Son loro che mi hanno avviato a pensarle cose che sono scritte in questo libro. Sui libri della scuola io non le avevo trovate. Le ho imparate mentre le scrivevo e le ho scritte perche' loro me le avevano messe nel cuore" (Milani, 1996, p. 76).

29. He was *troppo scomodo* (made one feel uncomfortable) to some of his superiors in the Church hierarchy with his rapier-thrust "talking back" and exacting attitude (his knowledge of languages, especially Hebrew, made him dispute textual interpretations). He had the temerity to show up some of his lecturers at the seminary for their perceived incompetence (Lancisi, 2007, p. 44). He would later mete out similar treatment to some of his invited speakers at San Donato (p. 69).
30. Scuola di Barbiana, 1996, p. 12.
31. Scuola di Barbiana, 1996, p. 82.
32. Scuola di Barbiana, 1996, p. 125.
33. Quite instructive here is the collective successful protest by the students for the building of a small bridge across a ditch on the way to Barbiana to prevent Luciano from falling as he made his way to the school from a distance (Gesualdi, 2008).

Chapter 4

1. See http://www.barbiana.it/LODI-MILANI.html.
2. Source: http://www.barbiana.it/biograf_adele.html ("Don Milani non mi diede mai consigli per la mia scuola, a parte la scrittura collettiva. Ma io non avevo coraggio. L'ho usata dopo anni che era morto e mi ha appassionato, perché i ragazzi partecipano. Quando facevo il tempo pieno, di pomeriggio, i ragazzi mi suggerivano sempre di fare scrittura collettiva")

References

A.A.V.V. (2007). "Don Milani e Paulo Freire: Due maestri del nostro tempo" (Don Milani and Paulo Freire: Two teachers of our time), numero monografico, *Lifelong lifewide learning*, anno II, n. 9.

Abbate, G. (2008). "La Scuola di Barbiana. Orientamenti e prospettive didattiche." In G. Abbate (Ed.), *Don Milani. Tra scuola e impegno civile.* Naples: Luciano Editore.

Allievi di San Donato and Lagomarsini, S. (2008). *Un libro inopportuno. Esperienze pastorali di Don Milani mezzo secolo dopo* (An inappropriate book. Pastoral experiences by Don Milani, half a century later). Firenze: Libreria Editrice Fiorentina.

Allman, P. (1996), "Freire with no dilutions" in Reno, H and Witte, M. (eds.), *37th Annual AERC Proceedings*, Tampa: University of South Florida.

Aprile, P. (2010). *Terroni. Tutto quello che è stato fatto perche gli Italiani del Sud diventassero Meridionali* (People who work the land. All that was made for Italians from the south to become southerners). Milan: Piemme.

Aprile, P. (2011). *Giu' al Sud. Perche i Terroni salveranno l'Italia* (Down south. Why the people who work the land will save Italy). Milan: Piemme.

Aronowitz, S. (1993). "Paulo Freire's Radical Humanism." In P. McLaren and P. Leonard (Eds.), *Paulo Freire. A critical encounter.* New York: Routledge.

Balducci, E. (1977). *Fede e Scelta Politica*, Milan: Mondadori.

Balducci, E. (2002). *L'insegnamento di don Lorenzo Milani*. Bari-Roma: Laterza.

Becchi, B. (2004). *Lassù a Barbiana ieri e oggi* (Up in Barbiana yesterday and today). Firenze: Polistampa.

Bencivinni, A. (2004). *Don Milani. Esperienza educativa, lingua, cultura e politica* (Don Milani: Educational, linguistic, cultural and political experience). Roma: Armando.
Bernardini, A. (1968). *Un anno a Pietralata*. Firenze: La Nuova Italia.
Bonanno, P. (2002). "The Process of Learning." In C. Bezzina, A. Camilleri Grima, D. Purchase, and R. Sultana (Eds.), *Inside secondary schools. A Maltese reader*. Malta: Indigo Books.
Borg, C. and Cardona, M (2008), Lorenzo Milani. L-Edukazzjoni u l-Ġustizzja Soċjali (Lorenzo Milani. Education and Social Justice), Malta: Media Centre Print.
Borg, C., Cardona, M., and Caruana, S. (2009). *Letter to a teacher. Lorenzo Milani's contribution to critical citizenship*. Malta: Agenda.
Borg, C., and Mayo, P. (2006). *Learning and social difference. Challenges for public education and critical pedagogy*. Boulder: Paradigm.
Borg, C., and Mayo, P. (2007). *Public intellectuals, radical democracy and social movements. A book of interviews*. New York: Peter Lang.
Bortone, M. (2008). *Tra parola e conflitto. La comunicazione in Don Lorenzo Milani* (Between word and conflict. Communication in Don Lorenzo Milani). Roma: Edizioni Universitarie Romane.
Bourdieu, P. (1976). "The school as a conservative force: Scholastic and cultural inequalities." In R. Dale, G. Esland, and M. Macdonald (Eds.), *Schooling and capitalism*, London: Routledge, Open University Press.
Bourdieu, P. (1970/1977). *Outline of a theory of practice*. Trans R. Nice. Cambridge, UK: Cambridge University Press.
Bourdieu, P. (1979/1984). *Distinction*. Trans R. Nice. Cambridge, MA: Harvard University Press.
Bourdieu, P., and Passeron J. C. (1977/1970). *Reproduction in education, society and culture*. Trans R. Nice. Beverly Hills, CA: Sage.
Bourdieu, P., and Passeron, J. C. (1990). *Reproduction in education, society and culture* (2nd edition), Newbury Park, CA: Sage.
Bruner, J. (1964). *On knowing—Essays for the left hand*. New York: Athenaeum.
Bruner J. (1985). *Child's talk: Learning to use language*. New York: Norton.
Bruner J. (1991). "The Narrative Construction of Reality." *Critical Inquiry 18* (Autumn 1991), *The University of Chicago*.
Burtchaell, J. T. (Ed.). (1988). *A just war no longer exists. The teaching and trial of Don Lorenzo Milani*. Notre Dame, Indiana: University of Notre Dame Press.
Cambi, F. (1995). *Storia della pedagogia*. Bari: Laterza.
Capanna, M. (2007). "Una 'Lettera' al Futuro" (A letter for the future). In M. Gesualdi (Ed.), *Scuola di Barbiana. Lettera a Une Professoressa. Quarnt' anni dopo*. Florence: Libreria Editrice Fiorentina.
Castiglione, A. (Ed.) (2004), *Danilo Dolci. Memory and Utopia*, Partinico: Centro per lo Sviluppo Creativo 'Danilo Dolci' (www.danilodolci.net)
Centro Formazione e Ricerca Don Lorenzo Milani e Scuola di Barbiana. (2008). *Socrate e*

Don Lorenzo (Socrates and Don Lorenzo). Vicchio (Florence): Centro Formazione e Ricerca Don Lorenzo Milani e Scuola di Barbiana.

Coccia N. (1967). "Riascoltiamo la voce di don Milani." *Avanti* (02/07/1967).

Corbi, E. and Sarracino, V. (1999), *Storia della scuola e delle istituzioni educative 1830–1999). La Cultura della Formazione* (History of the School and Educational institutions 1830–1999. The Culture of Education, Naples: Liguori,

Corradi, A. (2012). *Non so se don Lorenzo . . .* (I do not know whether Don Lorenzo . . .). Milan: Feltrinelli.

Corzo, J. L. (2011). "Alla Scuola della Parola. Analisi teologico-spirituale degli scritti di don Lorenzo Milani" (For the school of the word. A theological-spiritual analysis of Lorenzo Milani's writings). In R. Sani and D. Simeone (Eds.), *Don Lorenzo Milani e la Scuola della Parola. Analisi storica e prospettive pedagogiche* (Don Lorenzo Milani and the School of the Word. Historical analysis and pedagogical perspectives). Macerata: Edizioni Università di Macerata (eum).

Corzo Toral, J. L. (2008). *Lorenzo Milani. Analisi spirituale e interpretazione pedagogica.* Troina (EN): Servitium-Città Aperta.

Cristante, S. (2008). Preface. In M. Bortone, *Tra parola e conflitto. La comunicazione in Don Lorenzo Milani* (Between word and conflict. Communication in Don Lorenzo Milani). Roma: Edizioni Universitarie Romane.

De Salvo, D. (Ed.) (2011). *L'eredità pedagogica di Don Milani.* Quaderni di Intercultura Anno III/2011, Messina.

Dekadt, E. (1970). *Catholic radicals in Brazil.* Oxford: Oxford University Press.

Dewey, J. (1916/1966). *Democracy and education.* New York: Free Press.

Dunn, J. (1988). *The beginnings of social understanding.* Cambridge, MA: Harvard University Press.

Edelsky, C. (Ed.). (1999). *Making justice our project: Teachers working toward critical whole language practice.* Urbana, IL: National Council of Teachers of English.

Fallaci, N. (1993). *Vita del Prete Lorenzo Milani. Dalla parte dell'ultimo* (Life of the Priest Lorenzo Milani. On the side of those who are last). Milan: Biblioteca Universale Rizzoli.

Freire, P. (1970/1993). *Pedagogy of the oppressed* (20th anniv. ed.). New York: Continuum.

Freire, P. (1973). *Education for critical consciousness.* New York: Continuum.

Freire, P. (1985) *Politics of Education: culture, power, and liberation,* South Hadley, MA: Bergin & Garvey.

Freire, P. (1993). *Education for critical consciousness.* New York: Continuum.

Freire, P. (1994). *Pedagogy of the oppressed* (20th anniv. ed.). New York: Continuum.

Freire, P. (1994). *Pedagogy of hope.* New York: Continuum.

Freire, P. (1998a). *Teachers as cultural workers. Letters to those who dare teach.* Boulder: Westview Press.

Freire, P. (1998b). *Politics and education.* Los Angeles: UCLA Latin American Center Publications.

Freire, P., and Macedo, D. (1987). *Literacy: Reading the word and the world.* Boston, MA: Bergin & Garvey.

Freire, P. and Macedo, D. (1995). "A dialogue: culture, language and race" in *Harvard Educational Review*, Vol. 65, No. 3, 377–402.

Gadotti, M., Freire, P., and Guimarães, S. (1995). *Pedagogia: Dialogo e conflitto* (Pedagogy: Dialogue and conflict) (B. Bellanova and F. Telleri, Eds.). Torino: Societa' Editrice Internazionale.

Galea, S. (2010). "Min hi l-Għalliema fl-Ittra lil Waħda Għalliema mill-Iskola ta' Barbjana? Sehem in-Nisa fil-Professjoni tal-Għalliema." (Who is the teacher in *Letter To a Teacher* by the School of Barbiana. Women's role in the teaching profession). In C. Borg (Ed.), *Lorenzo Milani: Bejn Ilbierah u Llum* (Lorenzo Milani: Between yesterday and today). Malta: Horizons.

Geertz, C. (1983). *Local knowledge. Further essays in interpretive anthropology.* New York: Basic Books.

Gennari, M. (Ed.). (2008*). L'apocalisse di don Milani.* Milan: Libri Scheiwiller.

Gesualdi, F., and Corzo Toral, J. L. (1992). *Don Milani nella scrittura collettiva.* Torino: Edizioni Gruppo Abele.

Gesualdi, M. (Ed.). (2005). *Don Lorenzo Milani. La parola fa eguali. Il segreto della Scuola di Barbiana.* Fondazione Don Lorenzo Milani. Firenze: Libreria Editrice Fiorentina.

Gesualdi, M. (Ed.). (2007). *Scuola di Barbiana. Lettera a Une Professoressa. Quarnt' anni dopo* (School of Barbiana. Letter to a teacher. Forty years later). Florence: Libreria Editrice Fiorentina.

Gesualdi, M. (Ed.). (2008). *Il Ponte di Luciano a Barbiana* (Luciano's bridge at Barbiana). Florence: Libreria Editrice Fiorentina.

Gesualdi, M. (2011a). "L'obbedienza di don Lorenzo." In M. Gesualdi (Ed.), *L'obbedienza nella Chiesa* (Obedience in the church). Florence: Liberia Editrice Fiorentina.

Gesualdi, M. (Ed.). (2011b). *L'obbedienza nella Chiesa* (Obedience in the church). Florence: Liberia Editrice Fiorentina.

Gesualdi, S. (2007). "Come e' nata 'Lettera a Una Professoressa'" (How the letter to a teacher came about). In M. Gesualdi (Ed.), *Scuola di Barbiana. Lettera a Une Professoressa. Quarnt' anni dopo.* Florence: Libreria Editrice Fiorentina.

Giroux, H. (1985). "Introduction." In P. Freire, *The politics of education.* South Hadley, MA: Bergin & Garvey.

Giroux, H. (1988a). *Teachers as intellectuals.* South Hadley, MA: Bergin and Garvey.

Giroux, H. A. (1988b). Literacy and the pedagogy of voice and political empowerment. *Educational Theory,* 38: 61–75.

Giroux, H. A. (1991). *Postmodernism, feminism, and cultural politics: Redrawing educational boundaries.* SUNY series, teacher empowerment and school reform. Albany: State University of New York Press.

Giroux, H. A. (1992). *Border crossings: Cultural workers and the politics of education.* New York: Routledge.

Giroux, H. A. (1993). *Living dangerously: Multiculturalism and the politics of difference.* New York: Peter Lang.
Giroux, H. A. (2010). *Hearts of darkness. Torturing children in the war on terrorism.* Boulder, CO: Paradigm.
Giroux, H. A., and McLaren, P. (1994). *Between borders: Pedagogy and the politics of cultural studies.* New York: Routledge.
Gramsci, A. (1975). *Selections from the prison notebooks* (Ed. V. Gerratana) (four volumes). Turin: Einaudi.
Green, Pam (2001). "Critical literacy revisited." in Fehring, H. and Green, P., Eds. (2001). *Critical literacy: A collection of articles from the Australian Literacy Educators' Association.* Newark, Delaware: International Reading Association. pp. 7-13.
Guzzo, G. (1998). *Don Lorenzo Milani, un rivoluzionario, un santo, un profeta, un uomo* (Don Lorenzo Milani, a revolutionary, a saint, a prophet, a man). Soveria Mannelli (Catanzaro): Rubbettino Editore.
hooks, b. (1994). *Teaching to transgress.* New York: Routledge.
Hoyuelos, P. A. (2004). *Loris Malaguzzi. Biografia pedagogica.* Bergamo : Edizioni Junior.
Iser, W. (1974). *The implied reader. Patterns of communication in prose fiction from Bunyan to Beckett.* Baltimore and London: Johns Hopkins University Press.
Iser, W. (1989). *Prospecting: From reader response to literary anthropology.* Baltimore: Johns Hopkins University Press.
Labov, W. (1972). *Sociolinguistic patterns.* Philadelphia: University of Pennsylvania Press.
Lancisi, M. (2007). *Don Milani. La vita* (Don Milani. The life). Milan: Piemme.
Lave J., and Wenger, E. (1991). *Situated learning: Legitimate peripheral participation.* New York: Cambridge University Press.
Lazzarin, P. (2007). *Don Lorenzo Milani.* Padova: Edizioni Messaggero.
Lodi, M. (1970). *Il paese sbagliato. Diario di un'esperienza didattica*, (The Mistaken Country. Diary of a Didactic Experience) Turin: Einaudi.
Macedo, D. (1994), Preface. In P. McLaren and C. Lankshear (eds.), *Politics of Liberation. Paths from Freire*, London and New York: Routledge.
Martinelli, E. (2007). *Don Lorenzo Milani. Dall'motivo occasionale al motive profondo.* (Don Lorenzo Milani. From the occasional motive to the profound motive). Florence: Società Editrice Fiorentina.
Marx, K., and Engels, F. (1970). *The German ideology*, C.J. Arthur (ed.), London: Lawrence and Wishart.
Mayo, P. (2001). "'Remaining on the same side of the river.' A critical review of Paulo Freire's Later Works." *Review of Education/ Pedagogy/ Cultural Studies, 22*, 4, pp. 369–397.
Mayo, P. (2007). "Critical approaches to education in the work of Lorenzo Milani and Paulo Freire." In *Studies in Philosophy and Education, 26*, 6, pp. 525–544.
Mayo, P. (2011). "I contribute di don Lorenzo Milani e Paulo Freire per una pedagogia critica." In R. Sani and D. Simeone (Eds.), *Don Lorenzo Milani e la Scuola della Parola. Analisi storica e prospettive pedagogiche.* Macerata: Edizioni Università di Macerata (eum).

McLaren, P. (2005). *Capitalists & conquerors. A critical pedagogy against empire.* Lanham, MD: Rowman & Littlefield.

McLaren, P. (2006). *Life in schools. An introduction to critical pedagogy in the foundations of education* (5th ed.). Boston: Pearson.

Milani, L. (1957). *Esperienze pastorali* (Pastoral experiences). Firenze: Libreria Editrice Fiorentina.

Milani, L. (1965). *L'obbedienza non è più una virtù* (Obedience is no longer a virtue). Firenze, Libreria Editrice Fiorentina.

Milani, L. (1970). *Lettere di Don Lorenzo Milani. Priore di Barbiana* (Letters by Don Lorenzo Milani. Prior of Barbiana). Milan: Oscar Mondadori.

Milani, L. (1988a). "Letter of Don Lorenzo Milani to the Military Chaplains of Tuscany Who Signed the Communiqué' of 11 February 1965." (Ed. and trans. J. T. Burtchaell). In J. T. Burtchaell (Ed.), *A just war no longer exists. The teaching and trial of Don Lorenzo Milani.* Indiana: University of Notre Dame Press.

Milani, L. (1988b). "Milani's Letter to the Judges." (Ed. and trans. J. T. Burtchaell). In J. T. Burtchaell (Ed.), *A just war no longer exists. The teaching and trial of Don Lorenzo Milani.* Indiana: University of Notre Dame Press.

Milani, L. (1991). *L'Obbedienza Non è Più Una Virtù* (Obedience is no longer a virtue). Florence: Libreria Editrice Fiorentina.

Milani, L. (1996). *La Parola ai Poveri. Rilettura di Una Esperienza e di Una Testimonianza* (The poor have the word. Rereading of an experience and a testimony). Fossano: Editrice Esperienze.

Milani, L. (1997). *Lettere alla madre* (Letters to his mother). (Ed. G. Battelli.). Genova: Marietti.

Milani, L. (2001). *I care ancora* (I care again). (Ed. G. Pecorini.). Città di Castello, Emi.

Milani, L. (2004). *Una Lezione alla Scuola di Barbiana* (A lesson at the School of Barbiana). Florence: Libreria Editrice Fiorentina.

Milani, L. (2007a). *La ricreazione* (Recreation). Firenze: Libreria Editrice Fiorentina.

Milani, L. (2007b). *Lettere di don Lorenzo Milani priore di Barbiana* (Don Milani's Letters, Prior of Barbiana). (Ed. M. Gesualdi.) Cinisello Balsamo, San Paolo.

Milani, L., and Scuola di Barbiana. (1967). *Lettere a una professoressa* (Letter to a teacher). Firenze: Libreria Editrice Fiorentina.

Muspratt, S., Luke, A., and Freebody, P. (1997). *Constructing critical literacies.* Sydney: Allen & Unwin.

O'Cadiz, P., Wong, P. L., and Torres, C. A. (1997). *Education and democracy. Paulo Freire, social movements and educational reform in São Paulo.* Boulder: Westview Press.

Pasolini, P. (2008). "La cultura contadina della scuola di Barbiana." In M. Gennari (Ed.), *L'apocalisse di don Milani* (pp. 138–146). Milan: Libri Scheiwiller.

Pecorini, G. (1998). *Don Milani. Chi era Costui?* (Don Milani. Who was he?). Milan: Baldini & Castoldi.

Pucci, G. (2007). "Presentazione." In L. Milani, *La ricreazione.* Florence: Libreria Editrice Fiorentina.

Rodari, G. (1973/2001). *Grammatica della fantasia. Introduzione all'arte di inventare storie*. Torino: Einaudi.

Rorty, R. (1979). *Philosophy and the mirror of nature*. Princeton, NJ: Princeton University Press .

Salvadori, M. L. (1994) *Storia d'Italia e crisi di regime. Saggio sulla politica italiana 1861–1994*, (The History of Italy and the regime crisis. Essay on Italian politics 1861–1994), Bologna: Il Mulino,

Scuola di Barbiana. (1996). *Lettera a una professoressa* (Letter to a teacher). Florence: Libreria Editrice Fiorentina.

Sessi, F. (2008). *Il Segreto di Barbiana. La storia di don Lorenzo Mialni, sacerdote e maestro*. Venie: Marsilio.

Sidoti, B. (2002). "Mario Lodi e i suoi ragazzi. Fortuna e critica della scrittura collettiva." In *La Vita Scolastica*, 19 (July 2002). Firenze: Giunti.

Simeone, D. (1996). *Verso la Scuola di Barbiana. L'esperienza pastorale educativa di don Lorenzo Milani a S. Donato di Calenzano* (Towards the School of Barbiana. The Pastoral Experience of Don Lorenzo Milani at San Donato di Calenzano). San Pietro in Cariano (Verona): Il Segno dei Gabrielli Editori.

Smith, F. (2003). *Unspeakable acts: Unnatural practices*. Portsmouth, NH: Heinemann.

Starnone, D. (2007). "A Barbiana Scoppio' il '68" (The '68 movement started at Barbiana). In M. Gesualdi (Ed.), *Scuola di Barbiana. Lettera a Une Professoressa. Quarnt' anni dopo*. Florence: Libreria Editrice Fiorentina.

Stephens, J. (1992). *Language and ideology in children's fiction*. White Plains, NY: Longman.

Taylor, C. (1979). *Interpretation and the sciences of man*. In P. Rabinow and W. M. Sullivan (Eds.), *Interpretative social science: A reader*. Berkeley: University of California Press.

Taylor, C. (1989). *Sources of the self: The making of the modern identity*. Cambridge, UK: Cambridge University Press.

Taylor, P. V. (1993). *The texts of Paulo Freire*. Buckingham: Open University Press.

Toriello, F. (2008). "*Lettera a una professoressa* quarant' anni dopo. Una Lettura interculturale" (*Letter to a Teacher* 40 years later. An intercultural reading). In G. Abbate (Ed.), *Don Milani. Tra scuola e impegno civile* (Don Milani. Between school and civil engagement). Naples: Luciano Editore.

Toriello, F. (2012). *Paulo Freire, Enrico Smaldone, Lorenzo Milani. La passione per l'uomo. La speranza per un mondo diverso*, (Paulo Freire, Enrico Smaldone, Lorenzo Milani. The passion for human beings. The hope for a different world). Salerno: Editrice Gaia.

Van Sluys, K., Lewison, M., and Seely Flint, A. (2006). "Researching critical literacy: A critical study of analysis of classroom discourse." *Journal of Literacy Research* 38(2), 197–233.

Waugh, C. (2009). *Plebs. The lost legacy of independent working class education*. Occasional paper. Sheffield, UK: Post 16 Educator.

Wells, K., and West, C. (2010), " Race-Talk. A Conversation with Dr. Cornel West." Ohio: Kirwin Institute for the Study of Race and Ethnicity, The Ohio State University, http://www.race-talk.org/a-conversation-with-dr-cornel-west/ accessed 1 June 2013.

Williams, E. J. (2012). "Critical literacy. Postulating a historical and theoretical discourse." In E. J. Williams (Ed.), *Critical issues in literacy pedagogy. Notes from the trenches.* San Diego, CA: Cognella.

Young, M., and Muller, J. (2010). "Three educational scenarios for the future: Lessons from the sociology of knowledge." *European Journal of Education*, *45*, 1, pp. 11–27.

Name Index

Allman, P., 1, 68, 115
Althusser, L., 8
Anyon, J., 8
Apple, M., 1
Aprile, P., 64, 115
Arns, P. E., 5
Aronowitz, S., 56, 69, 115
Baudelot, C., 8
Bensi, R., 13, 15, 33, 34, 35, 39
Berlinguer, E., 56
Betto, F., 5, 55
Biondo, Il, 52
Boff, L., 5
Borg, C., 5, 6, 9, 50–51, 55–61, 65–67, 70, 72, 74, 76–78, 86, 112,116, 118
Bosco, D., 60
Bourdieu, P., 8, 67, 73, 76, 78, 84, 116
Boudon, R., 8
Bowles, S., 8
Brambilla, E., 75
Britzman, D., 1
Bruner, J., 81, 95, 96, 102, 116

Buber, M., 70, 72
Cabral, A., 62, 64
Cardona, M., 9, 50, 56–58, 61, 66, 67, 70, 72, 74, 76–78, 86, 116
Caruana, S., 9, 50, 56, 58, 61, 66, 67, 70, 72, 74, 76–78, 86, 116
Capitini, A., 2
Capanna, M., 8, 52, 53, 116
Carmichael, S., 59
Corradi, A.,43, 78, 102, 103, 111, 117
Corzo Toral, J., L 3, 54, 81, 82, 84, 96–102, 117, 118
Cossiga, F., 56
Dale, R., v, vii–ix, 111, 116
Dalla Costa, E., 30, 32
Darder, A., 1
Dewey, J., 1, 27, 28, 37, 53, 110, 117
Dolci, D., 2, 51, 54, 116
Don Milani *see* Milani, L.
Du Bois, W.E. B., 1
Establet, R., 8
Fallaci, N., 15, 35, 36, 39, 55, 67, 106, 117

Name Index

Ferrer i Guàrdia, F., 53
Freinet, C., 38, 44, 53
Freire, P., 1, 5, 7, 9, 51–57, 62, 65, 69, 71–76, 78, 83, 98, 101, 103–5, 111, 115, 117–19, 120, 121 Gadotti, M., 57, 118
Galastri, C., 55
Gentile, G., 72, 108
Gesualdi, F., 36, 42, 81, 82, 84, 96, 97, 98, 100, 101, 102, 118
Gesualdi, M., 42, 69, 75, 82, 92, 96, 112, 113, 116, 118
Gesualdi, S., 51, 52, 54, 57, 67, 118, 121
Gintis, H., 8
Giroux, H., 1, 2, 5, 6, 75, 78, 81, 83, 118, 119
Gomez, J. P., 2
Gozzini, Dott., 45, 73
Gramsci, A., 1, 2, 7, 55, 61, 62, 64, 65, 68, 70, 72, 73, 108, 119
Guimaraes, S., 57, 118
Guzzo, G., 57, 119
hooks, b., 1, 57, 119
Illich, I., 9
Kincheloe, J., 1
Lancaster, J., 74
Lenin, V. I., 70
Lodi, M., 2, 38, 43, 44, 54, 75, 84, 85, 86, 92, 96, 102, 103, 113, 119, 121
Lucchetti, D 53
Luciano, 89, 113, 118
Lyotard, J. C., 8
McLaren, P., 1, 6, 55, 83, 115, 119, 120
Martinelli, E., 6, 9, 56, 59, 60, 62, 64, 69, 70, 71, 72, 112, 119
Marx, K., 4, 7, 55, 57, 71, 119
Mazzolari, P., 39
Milani, A. (father), 11

Milani, A. (son), 105
Milani Comparetti, A., 67
Milani L. 1–9, 10–16, 20–49, 50–80, 81–87, 92, 94, 96–98, 100–104, 107–113, 115–121
Muller, J., 61, 122
Mussolini, B., 10, 11, 12, 13, 63
Nyerere, J. K., 62
O'Sullivan, E., 3
Pasolini, P.P., 8, 52, 60, 94, 95, 120
Passeron, J. C., 8, 67, 73, 77, 116
Pecorini, G., 43, 84, 120
Pipetta, 7, 22, 57
Plato, 7, 54
Poulantzas, N., 8
Rodari, G., 2, 38, 85, 101, 102, 103, 121
Rorty, R., 97, 121
Schugurensky, D., 3, 51, 111
Schweitzer, A., 59
Segni, P., 56
Shor, I., 1, 75
Simon, R.I., 1
Socrates, 7, 54, 104, 117
Starnone, D., 53, 121
Steinberg, S., 1
Taylor, C., 95, 97, 121
Taylor, P. V., 76, 121
Toriello, F., 60, 121
Tranquillo, 67
Urquhart, C., 59
Vanney, C., 51
Vygotsky, L., 1, 74, 84
Weil, S., 29
Weiss, A. (Mother), 12, 14–16, 29, 30, 33, 35, 41, 48, 49, 55, 105, 106, 107, 120
West, C., 5, 54, 121
Young, M., 61, 122

Subject Index

Abu Ghraib, 6
Against the grain, 6, 15, 64, 76
Agency, 78, 98
Apologia, 7, 54
Argentina, 3, 51

Banking education, 65, 72
Barbiana School, 33, 35, 41, 43–45, 54, 73, 77, 81, 83–85, 89, 95, 96, 102, 103
Basismo, 72
Being, 68–69
Bourgeois/ie, 4, 5, 7, 8, 54, 56, 59, 63, 65, 78, 82, 91, 92, 93, 94, 95, 96, 97, 108

Carnival balls, 56
Catcom, 112
Catholic Church, 4, 5, 12–14, 17, 19, 20–22, 28, 31, 33, 34, 39, 40, 43, 45, 47, 52, 54, 56, 71, 77, 88, 109, 110, 113, 118
Catholic University of the Sacro Cuore, 52
Centre for Leadership and Diversity 3
Centres for Social Orientation, 2

Centro Formazione e Ricerca Don Lorenzo Milani e Scuola di Barbiana, 54, 116
Christian, 4, 5, 23, 27, 45, 47, 54, 55, 64, 107, 109
Christian Democrat, 16, 17, 18, 19, 20, 32, 77, 107, 109, 110
Citizenship 49, 60, 66, 69, 75, 77, 116
Class analysis, 7
Class hierarchies, 65
Class identity, viii, 4
Class privileges, 63, 64
Class selection, viii
Class status, viii
Class struggle, 62
Class suicide, 62, 63, 64, 65
Classe dirigente, 76
Collective text, 43, 92, 95, 96
Colonialism / Colonisation, 22, 64
Community, 2, 24, 25, 28, 39, 53, 63, 68, 71, 75
Conferenza del venerdì (the Friday conference), 72

Subject Index

Conscientious objection, 5, 45, 46, 47, 51, 53, 54
Conscious direction, 65
Consumerism, 60, 61, 64
Controlling agents, 84
Constantinian Church, 5
Critical literacy, 76, 83, 97, 103, 119
Critical pedagogy, viii, 1–3, 5, 51, 54, 55, 57, 62, 72, 74–76, 81, 104, 105, 116, 120
Cultural arbitrary, 65
Cultural capital, 8, 61, 66, 67, 68

Debtocracy, 6
Democrazia Proletaria, 52
Dialectical relationship, 57
Dialogue/dialogical, 5, 17, 19, 28, 45, 72, 74, 82, 94, 103, 104, 118
Disobedience, 104
Dominant class, 5, 56
Don Camillo-Peppone series, 56
Doposcuola (after-school programme), 75, 79

Eastern Bloc, 56
Emancipation, 27
Empire, 5, 6, 10, 12, 63, 120
Equality, 31, 38, 50, 56, 59, 92
Escuela Moderna, 53
Ethiopia, 10, 12, 63
Evaluation, 26, 27, 44, 110
Exams, 12, 13, 23, 44, 64, 67, 70, 90, 93, 105, 106

Gender, 57, 58
Gianni bocciati (failed Giannis), 51, 57, 65–68, 70, 72, 85
Giornale Scuola, 2
Grammatica della fantasia (Grammar of Fantasy), 2, 121
Greeks, 70
Guantanamo, 6

Habitus, 8, 62, 65, 73, 77
Hegemony, 83, 84
Hermeneutic circle, 95, 96

Higher-order thinking, 79
Hiroshima, 7
History, 5, 6, 11, 12, 17, 22, 29, 46, 49, 58, 64, 67, 70, 76, 81, 85, 111, 117, 121

Ignorance, 23, 83, 97
Independent Working Class Education, 62, 121
Individualism, 8, 74, 75, 77, 93
Invisible pedagogies, 61
Italian constitution, 18, 37, 46, 48, 65, 66, 79, 110
Italian state, 12, 26, 27, 45, 53

Judges, 9, 10, 47, 50, 54, 58, 64, 66, 72, 76, 81, 82, 120
Klasse in sich / klasse für sich, 4
Knowledge, viii, 4, 5, 30, 44, 61, 62, 70, 74–76, 82–83, 91, 96–98, 110, 113, 118, 122 S)

Language teaching, 71
Latin America, 3, 51, 52, 55, 72, 117
League tables, 8
Letter to a Teacher (*Lettera*), vii, 3, 7, 9, 10, 14, 15, 21, 22, 24, 25, 29, 31, 33–36, 39, 40–42, 44–50, 57–58, 62, 64, 72–73, 75, 76, 81–88, 92, 94, 96, 99, 101–3, 106, 107, 111, 116–18, 120–21
Liberation Theology, 5, 52, 55

Magisterial school, 52, 57
Manifesto, Il, 53
Marxist/ism, 7, 8, 19, 52, 55, 109
Media, 5, 76, 79, 103, 116
Meritocracy, 66
Middle / bourgeois class, 11, 23, 33, 45, 61, 66, 91, 94, 106
Militarization, 5, 6, 7
Military chaplains, 9, 45–47, 50, 54, 59, 62, 64, 120
Military conscription, 51, 53, 54
Modernizing church, 5
Movimiento de Renovación Pedagógica de Educadores Milanianos, 3

Narrative structures, 81
Newspapers, 16, 22, 26, 46, 53, 85, 93

Ontario Institute for Studies in Education, 3
Omnicrazia, 2

Parents, viii, ix, 12–15, 36, 44–45, 54, 57–58, 66, 80, 84, 88–91, 96, 106
Partito dei laureati (graduates' political parties), 56, 64
Pastoral experiences, 7, 21, 22, 24, 26, 31, 32, 35, 38, 40, 43, 52, 64, 107, 115, 120
Patronizing treatment of Africans, 59
Paulo and Nita Freire International Project of Critical Pedagogy, 1
Peasants, 4, 61, 63, 70, 71, 74, 75, 82, 88, 91, 92
Pedagogy of the snail, 69
Peer tutoring, 5, 73, 74, 79
Performativity, 8
Poisonous gas, 63
Poor, the, 5, 38
Poor Christs (*Dolci*), 51
Power, 2, 4, 8, 10–12, 17, 18, 23, 28, 30, 42, 57, 59, 61, 63, 75, 81–83, 92–93, 103, 117, 118
Powerful knowledge, 4, 61
Praxis, 72, 79
Private tuition, 68
Prophetic church, 5

Race, 5, 59, 67, 118, 121
Reggio Emilia Municipality, 2
Resistance, 16, 17, 18, 24, 43, 68, 84
Risorgimento, 63, 64
Romans, 70
Ruling class, 4, 10, 11, 63, 76

School of social service, 58
Scuola dell'obbligo (the compulsory public school), 7, 54, 58, 59, 65, 68, 69, 70, 71, 72, 74, 76, 78, 79
Sessantotto ('68), 8, 9, 10, 52, 53, 121
Six-day War, 59

Social change, viii, 9, 83, 98, 103
Social class, 5, 24, 25, 37, 48, 58, 59, 63, 64, 67, 68, 73, 78, 84
Socialism, viii, 55, 56, 108
Sovereign citizen, 4, 77
Specialization, 67, 72
Standardisation, 8
Subaltern, 65, 76

Taxes/taxation, 61, 66, 92, 93
Teachers, 10, 13, 23, 25, 38, 44, 48, 58, 63, 66–69, 71, 73–74, 76, 78–80, 84, 89, 93, 95, 103, 109, 115, 117–118
Testing, 8
Theology, 3, 5, 52, 55
Trade unionists, 52, 93
Treblinka, 6
Truth, 20, 46, 54, 82, 94, 95, 97, 102, 112

UNESCO, 3

Vatican II Council, 5
Voice, 14–16, 22, 47, 54, 59, 73, 81, 100, 103, 108, 118

Word, 3, 5, 6, 23–25, 28–29, 31, 39, 42, 47, 56, 62, 70–72, 76, 78, 82, 86, 87, 90, 92, 94–96, 98, 100, 101, 103–4, 106, 116 118, 120
Workers, 1, 2, 18–19, 21, 23, 25, 32, 48–49, 52, 56, 61, 72, 74–75, 78, 82, 88, 91, 94, 117–18
Working class, 4, 13, 21, 24, 25, 26, 30, 33, 34, 56, 57, 61, 62, 70, 71, 77, 93, 121
World Council of Churches 52
Writing, 2–3, 6–8, 16, 20, 22, 27, 29, 38, 44, 53, 55–56, 58, 64, 67, 69
collective, 54, 75, 78, 81–104, 108, 117

Zones of Proximal Development, 74

About the Authors

Federico Batini is a researcher at the University of Perugia. Founder and director of a training and guidance agency Pratika (www.pratika.net) and the centre of ideas and cultural productions Nausika (www.narrazioni.it), he is also a senior partner of Thélème (www.theleme.it). He has been dealing with stories and narratives in many formats for the past twenty years. He is working on a project of books and audio books of fairy tales and fables rewritten and adapted in collaboration with modern writers and experts. He has written plays and short stories, edited anthologies and written lyrics. He has devised a method of guidance through story telling called narrative guidance (*Per un orientamento narrativo*, 2000) and has published articles, books, and other materials about this method. His most recent publications include *L'orientamento narrativo a scuola. Lavorare sulle competenze per l'orientamento dalla scuola dell'infanzia all'educazione degli adulti* (2008); *Mettere in circolo. Una ricerca sui circoli di studio: Dalla pratica al metodo* (2008); *Competenze e diritto all'apprendimento* (co-edited with A. Surian, 2008); *L'Isola sconosciuta. Un progetto di orientamento narrativo: Metodi e risultati, Storientando: Un progetto e una ricerca con l'orientamento narrativo* (with A. Surian, 2008); *Storie, futuro e controllo* (ed., 2011); *Storie e orientamento. Percorsi per l'orientamento narrativo di gruppo* (2011), *Orientare per non disperdere: le storie siamo noi*; *Quando i figli scelgono*

(2011); *Comprendere le differenze; Verso una pedagogia dell'identità sessuale* (2011); *Storie che crescono* (2011).

Peter Mayo is Professor in the Department of Education Studies, Faculty of Education, University of Malta. His many books include *Gramsci, Freire and Adult Education* (1999), subsequently published in translation in six languages; *Liberating Praxis* (2004), which won an AESA Critics Choice Award in 2005; *Learning and Social Difference* (with C. Borg, 2006); *Adult Education in Malta* (2007); *Public Intellectuals, Radical Democracy and Social Movements: A Book of Interviews* (with C. Borg, Peter Lang 2007); *Learning with Adults: A Critical Pedagogical Introduction* (with L. English, 2007), winner of the 2013 C. Houle Award for outstanding literature in adult education; *Politics of Indignation* (2012); and *Echoes from Freire for a Critically Engaged Pedagogy* (2013). He was 2011 winner of the CIES Higher Ed SIG award for best paper in comparative/international Higher Ed. He co-edits Palgrave Macmillan's book series on postcolonial studies in Education and edits the Sense book series on International Issues in Adult Education. He is co-editor of the refereed journal, *Postcolonial Directions in Education*.

Alessio Surian is researcher at the University of Padova where he teaches Transformative Learning. He is co-coordinator of the Special Interest Group on Teaching and Learning in Culturally Diverse Settings of the European Association for Research on Learning and Instruction and a member of the executive committee of the World Education Forum. He is the author of several studies on participatory methodologies, collaborative learning and intercultural communication, including "Mr. Palomar and Youth 2.0: Beyond the Faustian Bargain" (*Italian Journal of Sociology of Education*, 2013); "Transformative Learning and Youth Agency within Present and Future Urban Scenarios" (*Italian Journal of Sociology of Education*, 2011); *Making a Difference: Learning That Matters* (ed.), Diversity Youth Forum, Strasbourg, 2007; and *Traveling Cultural Diversity* (ed.), British Council–SALTO, London, 2005.

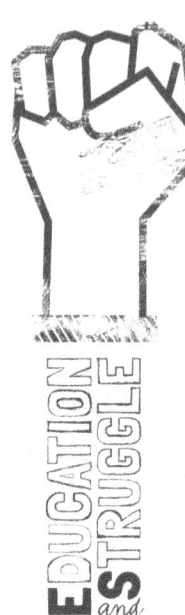

Narrative, Dialogue and the Political Production of Meaning

Michael A. Peters
Peter McLaren
Series Editors

To submit a manuscript or proposal for editorial consideration, please contact:

Dr. Peter McLaren
UCLA Los Angeles
School of Education &
Information Studies
Moore Hall 3022C
Los Angeles, CA 90095

Dr. Michael Peters
University of Waikato
P.O. Box 3105
Faculty of Education
Hamilton 3240
New Zealand

WE ARE THE STORIES WE TELL. The book series Education and Struggle focuses on conflict as a discursive process where people struggle for legitimacy and the narrative process becomes a political struggle for meaning. But this series will also include the voices of authors and activists who are involved in conflicts over material necessities in their communities, schools, places of worship, and public squares as part of an ongoing search for dignity, self-determination, and autonomy. This series focuses on conflict and struggle within the realm of educational politics based around a series of interrelated themes: indigenous struggles; Western-Islamic conflicts; globalization and the clash of worldviews; neo-liberalism as the war within; colonization and neocolonization; the coloniality of power and decolonial pedagogy; war and conflict; and the struggle for liberation. It publishes narrative accounts of specific struggles as well as theorizing "conflict narratives" and the political production of meaning in educational studies. During this time of global conflict and the crisis of capitalism, Education and Struggle promises to be on the cutting edge of social, cultural, educational, and political transformation.

Central to the series is the idea that language is a process of social, cultural, and class conflict. The aim is to focus on key semiotic, literary, and political concepts as a basis for a philosophy of language and culture where the underlying materialist philosophy of language and culture serves as the basis for the larger project that we might call dialogism (after Bakhtin's usage). As the late V.N. Volosinov suggests "Without signs there is no ideology," "Everything ideological possesses semiotic value," and "individual consciousness is a socio-ideological fact." It is a small step to claim, therefore, "consciousness itself can arise and become a viable fact only in the material embodiment of signs." This series is a vehicle for materialist semiotics in the narrative and dialogue of education and struggle.

To order other books in this series, please contact our Customer Service Department:

    (800) 770-LANG (within the U.S.)
    (212) 647-7706 (outside the U.S.)
    (212) 647-7707 FAX

Or browse online by series:

    www.peterlang.com

www.ingramcontent.com/pod-product-compliance
Ingram Content Group UK Ltd.
Pitfield, Milton Keynes, MK11 3LW, UK
UKHW022240230426
12048UKWH00018BA/1369